MINDFUL ENTREPRENEURSHIP

Insightful Business Management Philosophies and Practices for Success

MUSBAHU EL YAKUB

In memory of my grandfathers,

Alhaji Yakubu Shattima, a mindful entrepreneur

and

Alkali Abubakar Jakada, a mindful scholar

Acknowledgements

This book is a compilation of a series of weekly columns written for the Nigerian daily, the Daily Trust, by me along with my several other notes, writings, and speeches elsewhere. The Entrepreneur column in the Daily Trust and my other entrepreneurship writings are all aimed at educating young entrepreneurs as well as seniors starting entrepreneurship at some point in their lives in our environment.

My sincere appreciation goes to the Daily Trust newspaper Board and management for the opportunity and particularly the Editor-in-Chief and Deputy Editor in the persons of Naziru Mikailu and Stella Iyaji, respectively. My thanks to Prof. Kamal Aliyu for the linguistic review of the manuscript, and Istvan and Angie for the formatting of the manuscript and the book cover design, respectively. Peter Aderibigbe is the always-available, versatile assistant that could make things happen.

My uncle, Alhaji Shehu El Yakub, who never missed the weekly write-ups, urged me on. My family has simply just been there with me anywhere, anytime, and anyhow. I can never thank them enough. Besides the family's emotional support and patience, my son, Mahmud, helped with the graphics and illustrations while my daughter, Laila, is the competent home office administrator that also helped with the indexing.

Thank you.

Musbahu El Yakub

Foreword

As a developing country with a rapidly burgeoning population, one of Nigeria's options for growing its economy and taking people out of poverty is through the deep and wide return to core entrepreneurship. The rewards of entrepreneurship to individuals, communities and the nation are multifold. These mean we should put in all the effort needed to train our people in modern ways of succeeding in business.

The opportunities in information technology, agriculture, commerce and industry, and solid minerals as well as several other industries are infinite in our country. But as the author has mentioned in the Preface, we need to not only develop the knowledge and skills of our people but also the discipline required to succeed locally and compete internationally.

Currently, public sector employments have, understandably, narrowed because of the limits of expansion in the sector. Opportunities for paid employment in the private sector are, in the interim, also limited. Thankfully, our young entrepreneurs are doing admirably well such as in the creative industry. It behoves us to support them to attain more successes in other industries to motivate and inspire others amongst them.

It is quite interesting and commendable that successive governments in Nigeria, both at the federal and state levels, have been working assiduously hard to support entrepreneurship by providing tailwinds to willing entrepreneurs. Again, we should encourage our youth not only to seize these opportunities but to also be alive to the corresponding responsibilities by living up to their contractual commitments.

I commend the author for a great job well done. He took up the issues that are crucial in entrepreneurship and discussed them in simple language devoid of jargon and avoidable technicalities, yet without losing appropriate details. He started from the basics of the individual assessing themselves and being sure that they want to pursue a life in entrepreneurship and how passion for business can grow gradually. Issues of the quality of staff, funding, prioritisation, self-leadership, providing leadership, etc. have all been presented brilliantly and eloquently. The author did not leave out the reality that there are headwinds in business for which they must be ready to handle.

I strongly recommend this book to aspiring entrepreneurs along with those wishing to further develop themselves as well as to libraries and institutions.

Simon Aranonu
Executive Director
Bank of Industry, Nigeria
August 2022

Preface

Different people have different reasons for wanting to be in business. Maybe that is all you ever wanted to do. Or perhaps you have inherited a large sum from a deceased relative. Possibly, you have grown up in a family of entrepreneurs and know nothing else. Or maybe you are unable to get a paid *'nine to five'* job. It is also probable that you just lost your job or are planning to voluntarily retire or otherwise leave your paid job. Whatever your reason or reasons, for you to stand a good chance of success, you need to be not just comfortable but excited about the prospects of the life of entrepreneurship. Equally as important, you must understand certain business management issues and be effective in getting things done.

At the lowest level, the life of entrepreneurship can be highly rewarding to us as individuals. At a higher level, it is a service to humanity. Think about it, most of what the scientists and engineers develop can hardly be sustainably made widely available and affordable if there isn't a commercial model behind them. This is the challenge of entrepreneurship. However, business life can be full of heartaches, risks, pitfalls and challenges for which you should be ready and comfortable in handling.

Unwisely, a lot of people who aspire or are already planning to go into business get only obsessed with the 'good life' prospects that their business may offer: the cars, the beautiful house, the travels, etc. These are all desirous, but there are other foundational issues to be aware of. First, some things must be done before the chance to have nice cars and a beautiful house can be realized. Second, there are sacrifices, difficulties and challenges that are also strewn along the path. For these two reasons, three things should be the preoccupation of the aspiring businessperson, instead.

What value can I add to my potential customers and other stakeholders? The business you go into is simply a vehicle on which this value is delivered. Unless the business does it to the satisfaction of the stakeholders and profitably to you, you are not in business.

What are the resources and skills that you and your people need to be able to deliver value to your potential customers and how can you provide those resources and attract those skills?

What are your situational peculiarities and how can you contextualise otherwise universal principles to your environment?

This book is about understanding the issues you have to think through and handle if you are to succeed in entrepreneurship.

Musbahu El Yakub
August 2022

Contents

Chapter 1

"The journey of a thousand miles begins with one step." - Lao Tzu

1.0 A Day in an Entrepreneur's Life

You woke up at 3 a.m. to review documents, send e-mails and think through how to raise the N20 million for the additional working capital required by the factory. There is a global squeeze on credits and raising funds is particularly difficult for you as a small-scale businessperson. Oh, then there are the children's school fees of N2.6 million to be paid as well. You have less than N100,000.00 on hand and in the bank.

By 7 a.m. you have taken breakfast and set out to the factory. The operatives desperately need working capital. You have scheduled a series of meetings to attend to after inspecting operations to 11 a.m. You return to the factory at 5 p.m. with no commitment from financiers on your financial need. You review the production for the day and set out to close at 8 p.m.

On your way home, you got a phone call from a prospective client informing you that your contract bid meeting has been slated for 9 a.m. the following morning, five hundred kilometres away. Your mind races through the options. The return air ticket will cost you a minimum of N80,000.00 and you don't have the cash on you. Even if you do, the first flight out of your city the next morning will not take you to the client's before 9 a.m.

Having made a decision, you call your spouse to set up your travel bag. As your bag is always sixty per cent packed for such trips, your spouse can put the add-ons pretty quickly. You got home at about 9 p.m., pick up your bag and set out to drive the five hundred kilometres.

It is the days of militant insurgency in the region and the roads are manned every few kilometres by armed security. The normally five-hour drive takes you seven, arriving at the client's town at 4 a.m. You check into your hotel and take a short nap from 5.30 and 7 a.m.

By 8.30 a.m. you are at the client's office and the session starts at 9.30 am. Having gone through the process with other competing companies, it was concluded by noon.

You lost the bid.

During the bid session, the factory had sent you an SMS that they were running out of fuel for production. You, therefore, need to meet with fuel suppliers to arrange for some supply on credit. You immediately hit the road on the return journey, arriving back at your city by 6 p.m., just in time to meet with the fuel suppliers. They decline your request. Production shutdown is imminent the following day unless you are able to secure fuel supply before 10 a.m. the following morning.

Do you think this is hypothetical? No. It happened to me. It is life in business.

I slept well that night, waking up early the following morning to take issues up again.

On several other good days, the orders come in from customers. The machines work supremely well. All employees are hands-on and the goods get delivered on time and to the satisfaction of the customers. We get paid. We pay our workers and suppliers. We are able to take the family on holiday. We support the local primary school in our community, and we pay our taxes.

Welcome to entrepreneurship.

2.0 Purpose and Mindset

After the arrival of the colonial masters to various parts of what later became Nigeria and the beginning of the introduction of Western-style public administration, the need for trained 'native' public servants began. With the increasing need for various services, the vacancies for trained manpower continued to balloon for several decades up to the 1980s. But by the late 1980s, we had begun not only to saturate the public services but probably over-employed. If any realistic and prudent thing is to happen to our public services over the next one decade, it should be a deliberate and systemic 'rightsizing'. That is a polite way of saying *downsizing* except probably for the military, the police, and other such services. Yes, obviously people will die or retire and there will be the need to employ replacements and for some marginal growth as well. But those combined vacancies are unlikely to meet up with the rate graduates from high schools and universities are churning out from all around the country. We have, therefore, not only to accept the reality that the public sector is never meant to be there just to employ graduates but also to gladly accept the truism that the public sector should, instead, focus on developing the enabling environment that will see to the creation and growth of businesses of all sizes in all the sectors and crannies of the country.

If you ask me, successive federal governments in the past have done reasonably well in encouraging graduates to go into self-employment and business through programs with the Bank of Agriculture, Bank of Industry, SMEDAN, NDE, NIRSAL, etc. But the call has not been sufficiently loud and unequivocal: Government should cease creating any impressions that it can directly employ the multitudes of our youth by honestly and clearly communicating that there are limited employment opportunities in the public sector that can come up from time to time. Instead, the government should continue to focus on strengthening the various interventionist and enabling programs that will facilitate the creation of employment by the youth themselves. Obviously, all the aforementioned programs can only succeed and be sustainable if responsibility of accountability is inculcated and enforced in our youth.

With a population of over two hundred million people and growing, there are more than sufficient local markets for many products and services. From abundant fertile land for agriculture across the country to solid minerals in most states of the federation, information technology, manufacturing and services, we really are literally a bottomless pit of opportunities for serious entrepreneurs. In the next pages, I would endeavour to bring out topical issues on entrepreneurship that will help our youth in understanding opportunities and how to seize them and create jobs for themselves and others.

The starting points for the success of any and every worthy endeavour in life are two: purpose and mindset.

One of the reasons many people fail to achieve meaningful and sustainable success in business and life is because they fail to identify their life's purpose from the get-go. Even when they can boast of what might seem to be reasonable outwardly achievements, they may still lack the full internal satisfaction necessary to keep them motivated and going for the marathon this life is. Lack of purpose costs us resources, such as our time, finances, efforts, relationships, etc. In the long run, we realise that it has deprived us of true meaning in the various spheres of our lives and the contentment that comes with it. Without a purpose or with a weak one, an individual can easily be swayed away from their otherwise noble journey. Entrepreneurship is particularly challenging.

The next crucial thing after 'purpose' is your *mindset*.

Consciously or subconsciously, everything starts with our mindsets. Successful entrepreneurs have an amazing perception of what they want to achieve years and even decades before it becomes reality. It is the clarity of the vision in their minds that keeps them highly motivated internally and quite relentless on the outside. And so, nothing seems to be able to stop them.

In the conceptual development and production of the 'Snow White and the Seven Dwarfs', the American, Walt Disney, faced unbelievable resistance from financiers, contributors, and other associates, including his brother, Roy Disney. Hollywood celebrities referred to the project as 'Disney's Folly'. But Disney was lucid in his mind as to what he wanted to achieve. He refused to lose focus on his desired outcome. In the end, the project cost a whopping 1.5 million in 1938 US dollars. But in the first weekend of its release, Snow White brought in $8 million, representing about $134 million in current dollars!

This level of confidence is never accidental. It is a consequence of a mindset that is committed to achieving identified objectives. Ask any successful entrepreneur, they will identify with this story of vision, mindset, and resolve.

With a clear purpose and a committed mindset, the next important thing the budding entrepreneur should be aware of is what to expect in entrepreneurship.

3.0 What to Expect on the Journey

An entrepreneurship journey could be prompted by different circumstances. Perhaps we have a 'one-in-the-world' business idea, or we have graduated from university and no job offers are forthcoming or maybe there are some government intervention programs in agriculture that excite us or yet still, we are about to retire and need to start some business to augment our retirement benefits.

Regardless of what is getting us into business, we have to think seriously about it; what to expect of it and what to prepare for. So, what are some of the things we should be aware of?

There is no opening or closing time and there are no 'weekends': There are always pleasant and not-so-pleasant surprises in the entrepreneurship journey. Opportunities and threats would often knock at any time without regard to your 'convenience', prior plans or schedule. The entrepreneurs that succeed are those that handle 'surprises' as they arise by ensuring that the pleasant ones are converted into realisable opportunities while the not-so-pleasant are controlled and any likely damage therefrom mitigated.

You can make money and you can lose money, too! Entrepreneurship is a great and fascinating way to make money. But making and losing money are two 'rigged' sides of the same coin. 'Rigged' because there are statistically more ways to lose than make money in most transactions and businesses. Consequently, the successful entrepreneur must think smart and work extra hard to overcome the losing odds and convert the winning chances.

There will be sleepless nights: An entrepreneur will always face some sorts of challenges. Challenges could come externally from customers, competition, government regulators, financiers, etc. Challenges could also be internal from your staff, product quality, etc. Whatever the challenges, successful entrepreneurs are always ready to address them before or as they come up.

There are no limits: Entrepreneurship is thrilling, even compulsive, to those who can face and take up challenges. You can explore your legitimate ideas without anyone stopping you. You can help solve problems that bother you or others and make money out of it. Over and beyond the fun you can have and the money you can make, entrepreneurship offers you boundless opportunities to change people's lives for the better. In entrepreneurship, the sky is not a limit!

Every outcome is a success: Successful entrepreneurs have some contrarian thinking. For instance, an entrepreneur may consider as a success what most of humanity would consider a failure. When Elon Musk launched an experiment, their Starship prototype rocket ended up exploding into smithereens when it was expected to land back on Earth intact and safely. Most people would consider the $100 million experiment a costly failure but not Mr. Musk. As far as he was concerned, the massive data they got from the experiment would make future attempts a success. He even made a joke of the 'failure', "*at least the crater is in the right place!*" That is an entrepreneurial mind for you.

It is now clear that there will be both opportunities and challenges on the journey. So, how do you prepare yourself to make the best and most of each for the greatest financial and non-financial benefits at minimum emotional stresses?

Beyond purpose and mindset that we discussed earlier, two other factors are also necessary:

Planning: Whenever you are travelling, it goes without saying that you will pack your bag with the stuff that you need for the period you will be on the journey. Where there will be weather issues, you ensure that you have the right clothes and shoes for the city you will be visiting. You would plan for the funds you need to pay for your passage, accommodation, local travels, feeding, gifts, etc. Similarly, before embarking on an entrepreneurship journey, you must plan ahead and in detail *what you want to achieve* and *how you want to achieve them*. This is called planning and it may be a stretch, but it must be implementable.

Identifying Required Resources: A critical component of planning that needs a separate mention is identifying the resources that will be required for your business. Resources might include personnel, funds, equipment, approvals and licenses, etc. For each resource, you will need to know what quantum of it is required, when it is required where and by whom. You should also know specifically how each will be acquired. *Our country is littered with many business ventures that have been abandoned at some stage, not because the business itself is not viable but because the promoters, for whatever reason, have not been able to provide some required resources to take it to success. In the end, they may end up forgoing a billion Naira sunk investment because they could not raise one hundred million Naira more!* 'Abandoned' businesses and projects are wasteful capital tie-up that do not make any returns and are at the risk of depreciating into worthlessness.

The small, medium and large local companies that you see and admire are the ongoing results of continuous anticipation, planning and execution by relentless entrepreneurs. You too can start from wherever you are now.

Figure 3.1: Mountaineers
(Image Credit: Sergio Cerrato - Italia from Pixabay)

Chapter 2

"A journey of a thousand miles continues with the second step." - Larry Wall

4.0 Mapping the Environment for Opportunities

The first practical step into entrepreneurship is coming up with a business idea. Searching for entrepreneurial opportunities is fundamentally about identifying either a deficiency or an inefficiency in a market. The object is to come up with an idea that can eliminate the deficiency or reduce the inefficiency by creating value that the target customers are willing to pay for at a profit to the entrepreneur.

There are two crucial rules for coming up with business ideas:

Rule Number One, understand the dynamics of demand and supply: At the end of everything, businesses are about selling some product (good or service). Consequently, all great business ideas are, somehow, about either meeting up with supply shortfalls or creating new demands. Hence, to come up with an idea that will meet commercial viability tests, you need to understand the dynamics or projections of the supply and demand of any existing or new product in any existing or to-be-developed market. The box below typifies the opportunity windows in any business.

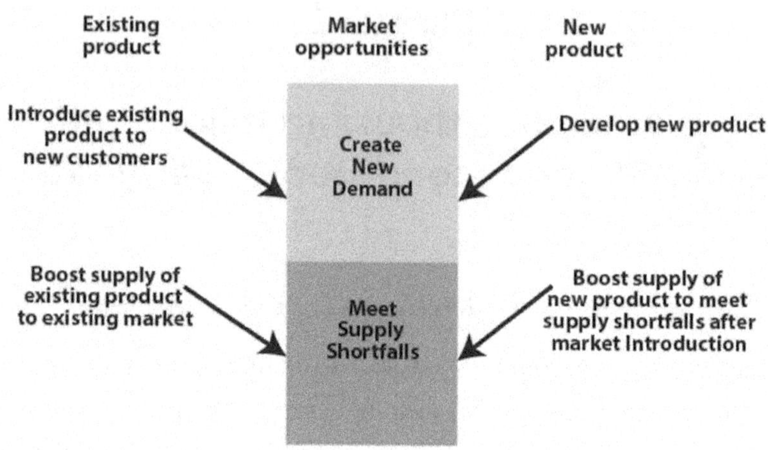

Figure 4.1: Market Opportunity Windows
(© Musbahu El Yakub)

In the mid-1980s, some entrepreneurs detected a decline in the purchasing power of the Nigerian middle-class. With a weakening purchasing power, the middle-class couldn't afford to purchase new motor vehicles as they easily used to. Those entrepreneurs seized the 'opportunity' and went into the importation of 'tokunbo' (used vehicles) that became affordable alternatives to the middle-class.

Rule Number Two, be alert: In the search for business ideas, nothing beats being alert. Ideas could come while discussing with a first-met passenger seated next to you on a short-haul flight. It could come during a supply chain meeting with senior corporate executives in your industry. Sometimes other people just deliberately or unwittingly tell us about business opportunities. Whichever way they come, we have to be alert to detect opportunities.

One of the best businesses I had was the importation of computer parts. It was in the early 1990s and laptops were still uncommon in Nigeria. I went to an IT shop to buy a memory card to upgrade my laptop and the shop attendant innocently and casually mentioned to me that the product was selling massively well but that their boss wasn't importing enough of them. I asked more questions, made some contacts and within two weeks I was on a flight to Singapore with borrowed cash from a benefactor to import the components.

After the rules, then some of the ways of coming up with business ideas:

What new thing can you do or what old ways can you do better? An entrepreneur can come up with a new product that is 'out of this world'. Sony's Walkman is an example of product that was conceptualised and developed reasonably from the ground up. It became one of Sony's most successful products and paved the way for later developments into mini-disc, MP3 and streaming music.

But more often than novel innovations, successful businesses just take an existing proposition and improve upon it. The improvement might be about providing some unmet needs of customers, such as convenience or safety in an already existing market. Examples are Amazon and Uber that introduced more convenient ways of serving existing markets by leveraging existing technologies.

Network, listen and ask questions: Business ideas are discussed by people every day. Being with the right people will expose you to great business opportunities being freely discussed. Similarly, attending trade fairs, conferences, industrial shows, etc. can uncover possible business ideas to you.

For those already employed, they get the opportunity to hear about business opportunities every day. It could be at discussions with colleagues, customers or suppliers. Whatever opportunity you may pursue in this line though, ensure that you do not do anything unethical or in violation of any contractual obligation you are bound to.

What do you and others spend money on? Looking at what you and others spend your money on can give you ideas on possible business opportunities. For example, individuals and corporations in Nigeria have been spending billions of Naira annually on mobile phones and related services over the last two decades. Similarly, where governments channel their funding into could lead you to business opportunities. For instance, over the last several years, successive administrations have pumped substantial funds into information technology and agriculture. IT shops, rice milling, etc, have grown rapidly over those years. What part of some chain can you add value to?

Create market niches: Sometimes markets can get too large or wieldy. When markets are large or wieldy, some deserving customers might not receive the value they expect or are entitled to. As an entrepreneur, you can carve out a segment of such markets and work to serve it better.

The 'no-frills' airlines are a good example of market segmentation. The no-frills provide what other discerning passengers may call cheap air travel services, but their loyal passengers accept what they pay for and get. Ryanair, a leading no-frills, has been, overall, more profitable than many conventional airlines. You too can carve out a market segment and make it 'yours'!

Search your areas of interest: It can be tricky trying to turn 'passions' into a business. I don't encourage it unconditionally. Instead, I insist that *as with all other business opportunities, you should only go into your areas of interest as a business if all the economic fundamentals indicate commercial viability.* I also tell people that for most entrepreneurs, the love and passion for what they do tend to increase as the success in their businesses increases with time. I, for one, never had any 'passion' for any computer parts when I saw an opening and commenced the business. But the money I started to make, the travels, the negotiations, the highs and the lows all made me love the computer and its parts! The point is we can stumble upon opportunities 'by accident' and the love and passion for them will grow when we begin to enjoy all that their business entail.

Having said that, some of our personal interests can pass the tests of feasibility. Microsoft was started by the duo of Bill Gates and Paul Allen on the strength of their passion for coding. But their commercial success was made possible only by the emerging possibilities for the common use of computers. So, you too can list down your core areas of interest and dispassionately assess the viability of each.

What are your areas of competence? In the same way, we can get viable business ideas from our areas of interest, we could also from our areas of strengths and competence. For instance, a brilliant agricultural engineering graduate can consider going into the design and local fabrication of agricultural implements and equipment to substitute for their importation in an unfavourable exchange rate regime. In the previous sixty years, great comedians have entertained Nigerians on television and at theatres nationwide almost for free. In the last two decades, however, young people with the requisite talent and skills have created a working model of entertaining people as stand-up comedians and Masters of Ceremonies with resultant financial benefits to them.

As with areas of interest, you must ensure that your areas of competence, in which you want to go into business, will be commercially viable.

Understand trends: Most successful businesses are about some 'new' things coming up, either on the demand or supply side of the market. On the other hand, many faltering businesses are about some 'old' things dying out. So, understanding specific trends can give you clues to emerging business opportunities as well as where threats lurk in existing ones. For instance, over the last few decades, there have been growing global concerns about the use of 'dirty' energy sources. But in Nigeria, beyond their use for environmental purposes, 'clean' energy sources such as solar, have been relief alternatives for the supply of electricity to households, offices and even public assets. The entrepreneurs that saw this trend ahead and acted on it have been doing reasonably well.

Open your eyes and mind in the markets: All products end up at some markets where they are sold. Being alert in markets can expose you to various products and their current limitations as well as the customers and their current frustrations. Market information on prices, volumes, quality requirements, deliveries, etc. is empirical proof of the success or failure of any product at any point in time. In particular, customer complaints are pointers to assured ways of getting initial basic information about possible opportunities.

Search the internet: Information has never come easier. Surfing the internet is another way of coming up with ideas. Online marketplaces offer a lot of reasonably dispassionate information about goods and services that brick-and-mortar markets may not provide. Product reviews and trends, market statistics, etc. that are on the internet can all give you a sense of what is happening to specific products in particular markets. But as with all other idea sources also, they must be analysed in the context of your local situations through tests of feasibility.

Other options: Other options of going into business are simply by buying into licences. For instance, many franchisors in various services offer franchisees the opportunity to buy into a working business model that has been tested and proven. Becoming a franchisee is a quick way to enter a market and learn several things to do with running a business under the guidance of an experienced franchisor. Similarly, Uber entrepreneurs with a fleet of vehicles and Agency Banking are ways of getting into businesses on the platforms of principals that offer opportunities.

Business ideas that could turn into positive opportunities are usually about some growing trends, solving some problems, improving less-than-ideal circumstances, etc. Converting a positive opportunity into a commercial success is about observation, thoughtful analysis, innovation, creativity and persistent execution. So, after coming up with a seemingly brilliant business idea, your next challenge will be to test its commercial feasibility.

5.0 Testing the Feasibility of a Business Idea

From the moment a 'go' decision is given to a business idea, substantial funds and physical and intellectual efforts, as well as emotions, are poured into it. The failure of a business idea to be transformed into a successful business is, therefore, costly on many dimensions. To minimise the risks of those possible but avoidable losses, it is imperative that a business idea is tested on the potentialities of its commercial feasibility before that 'go' decision is given. Of the many other benefits of conducting a feasibility study are that it points out the valid bases of going on with a business idea in an informed, clear, intelligent and logical way. It narrows down diverse business options, thereby creating focus. It brings to light the kind of success that may be achievable over a period of time, etc.

Before we go into how a business idea could be tested for its latent commercial success, we need to first understand that there is a difference between a business feasibility study and a business plan, which two are often confused or mixed up by many. A feasibility study is basically to help to determine whether or not a business idea stands an acceptable chance of viability or not. A feasibility study would, typically, bring out facts, analysis, projections, conditions and limitations for the success of a business idea while a business plan will bring out the chosen tactics and strategies required to achieve a target business success and growth. If an idea is determined to be not feasible, the need for a business plan is immediately precluded.

Having said that, I like to group the tests of business feasibility into 'product tests', 'market conditions', 'financial conditions', 'resource tests' and 'risk analysis'.

Product Tests: These are all the tests in which you will establish certain fundamentals about your product (good or service) offering. What are the benefits of the product to your target market? At what price can you place the product in the market? Are there competing substitutes that can partly or completely replace your product? If there are, why should customers patronise you and your product and not the competition and their substitutes? How are similar and substitute products doing in the markets? Etc.

In conducting these checks, it is compulsory that the entrepreneur isolates and eliminates their sentiments, desires and hopes about the product from its actual value that the potential customer perceives and is willing to pay for.

Market Conditions: All economic factors are essential to business success. In particular, however, market conditions are fundamental. Who are the customers you wish to serve? What are the demographics of your customers and where are they located? What are the economic and social statuses of your customers? Can the customers afford the price of the product that makes the business profitable? Will the market grow or shrink in the years to come? How is the competition doing and why? Etc.

Financial Conditions: Finance is the lubrication of the moving parts of a business. Once a business idea will not be financially viable, it is considered 'dead before arrival'. So, the entrepreneur must be sure of some financial parameters before launching their business. Can you raise, internally and/or externally, the funds required for the purchase of assets and the ongoing operations of the business? What will be your fixed and variable costs? How quickly will breakeven be achieved? How strong is the cash flow forecast? Etc.

Resource Tests: All businesses require certain resources to operate and succeed. Unless those resources are provided in, at least, certain minimum quantities and at the time they are required, the business will be jeopardized. Hence, for any business idea to be transformed into business success, you need to answer questions like: Can you provide the required funds for the take-off and continuous operations? Is the technology available for your business and its operations? Can you get the equipment, software, etc. the business will require? Will you have the skilled and non-skilled manpower you need? Will the existing local, national and/or international infrastructure support or militate against the business? Etc.

Risk Analysis: One of the great misconceptions many people have is that 'business is about taking risks'. Really, nothing can be farther from the truth! Rather, savvy businessmen and women are curious about and alert to the risks each transaction or business may portend. Consequently, they first identify and assess the risks associated with the business both on one-off and/or continuous basis. Like the other tests and conditions above, risks will need to be assessed along various pertinent dimensions, such as market, finance, resources, etc. After identification and assessment, mitigation and control measures must be put in place wherever necessary.

So far, what we have discussed are the *benefits* of conducting a business feasibility study, the *difference* between a feasibility study and a business plan and the *issues* that a feasibility study grapples with. However, we have really not discussed *how* a feasibility study can be conducted. For instance, how do you establish if a price that will be profitable to the company will be accepted by the customers?

Next will be 'the *how*' of testing variables in a feasibility study. We want to see how information can be obtained and specific tests conducted. For constraints of space, we will consider only a few market and financial variables.

The tests of business feasibility start with the entrepreneur raising questions that must be answered to ascertain the viability status of a business concept. The questions will cut across all the dimensions discussed earlier. The more pointed questions you ask and the better answers you can get, the better will be the quality and reliability of the test results.

Market questions that are to be answered may include, what is the size of the market? Is the market growing or shrinking and at what rate? Can your potential customers afford the selling price of the product? What is the competition doing? Etc. Financial questions can include, what amount of funds do you require and for what? What will be your production costs? At what volume and when will the business breakeven? Etc. To answer these questions, you will need to do a lot of physical and dispassionate intellectual work.

Market information: Generally, market size can be established from industry reports and the annual accounts of companies doing the same business that reveal revenue volumes and market share. Market growth rates can be estimated from demographic reports and economic indicators from the National Bureau of Statistics and the Central Bank of Nigeria. To find out if target customers will pay the price that you will be offering, you can check the prices of competing products and their corresponding sales volumes. Similarly, you can conduct direct surveys asking pertinent questions to the target customers.

If you, for instance, want to open a restaurant at a working area like Broad Street, Lagos or Adetokumbo Ademola, Wuse II, Abuja, you will need to make footprint and drive-in estimates at various times of the day and various days of the week at about the location you want to operate. You should also try to get the estimates of online orders that nearby, operating restaurants take. To understand the competition, visit other restaurants in the area and see what they are doing and how they are doing it. Who are their customers? What is on their menu? How is the food quality? What are their prices? What other services do they offer? You can also survey their customers to understand what attracts them to the restaurants and what other services will fancy them.

Financial information: A start-up entrepreneur will need to establish their costs of equipment, raw materials, staff salaries, utilities, etc. The appropriate way to do this is to check with various suppliers of the equipment and raw materials, so that you can get the actual costs. Fluctuations in raw material costs can and do ruin many businesses. It is, therefore, necessary to get historical costs, seasonal fluctuations and future projections from experienced salespersons, consultants and advisors in the trade.

You can estimate your likely staff costs first by establishing what staff vacancies you need to fill and the salaries and other benefits that such staff earn in the industry. You can get salary estimates from recruitment agencies as well as employees working in the industry. Energy costs are critical in Nigeria. You will need to know the power consumption of all the equipment you need, how long they will operate daily and the current electricity tariff from your local distribution company. Where an auxiliary power plant will be used, you must know its fuel consumption rate and fuel costs per appropriate unit of measure.

These exercises and more will reveal to you the costs of equipment as well as the material, labour and overheads that will make up your unit production costs. Having determined what selling price your target customers will willingly pay, you can work out your breakeven volumes, profitability, etc. You can then make projections into the near future with the appropriate market growth rates and other economic indicators.

At the end, the information you get from your must-be-detailed surveys and studies is what you will analyse to understand the overall status of the idea. Unless where friends and family are professionally competent on a matter or where they are potential paying customers, their opinions must only be taken lightly because they will most likely not be dispassionate with you. On the other hand, you should consider engaging a reliable, trusted and competent senior or mentor who 'has been there done that' to help you to interpret the information and data independently for second opinions. Regardless of the opinions of everyone though, remember that you are ultimately responsible for your idea, its quality and success. It is perfectly possible that you see and believe in certain things that make the idea viable, but others do not.

6.0 Business Modelling

Creating and delivering value in ways desired and accepted and for which customers are willing to pay a price that is profitable to you is key to business success. The vehicle that we can provide and through which we compete well against others to create and deliver value to our customers is our business model. Business modelling, the process of developing a business model, is our subject now.

What is business modelling? The process of conceptualising, designing and developing an operating model for your business is called business modelling. The objective of a business modelling process is to come up with an operating platform and process that puts your business ahead of the competition by providing desired value to your customers and at acceptable costs and profits to you. The end result of a business modelling process is the creation of a business model. A business model could be 'greenfield' or adopted, adapted, modified or updated from an existing one, as may be required. No matter, a business model should just leverage the application of effort and use of other resources to achieve corporate goals in a competitive environment. Joan Magretta says that a business model *"..is the story that explains how an enterprise works."*

The importance of having the 'right' business model: A business model is both the core strategy as well as the heart of the value proposition of your business. It is what makes it possible for you to deliver on your value proposition. It is required to crack open new markets as well as grow existing ones. You need the right model to seize opportunities as well as address challenges. A business model is one of the first attributes that attract investors and excite initial staff to be engaged. Similarly, creditors who may provide funding will be interested in how effective and efficient your model is in delivering value to target customers.

The features of great business models: Knowingly or unknowingly, every business operates on some model. But to achieve your objectives, you are to consciously develop your model by making the right policy and asset choices along the following lines:

- Innovative: A business model must be innovative in terms of how you plan to create value, deliver value and beat competition.

- Demand generation: Your business model must create demand for your products.

- Proactive to competition: The business model you develop should take into consideration what the competitors are doing or likely to do and beat them at it.

- Profitable: At the end of everything, your model is to make your operations profitable.

- Clear processes: A business model has to be lucid in its processes, leaving no room for ambiguity and confusion.

- Resource types and utilisation: A business model that will work has to be clear on resources required, mode of acquisition and utilisation. Specifically, you must be able to provide the human capital and technology that may be required.

- Simple and Executable: The best things in business tend to be simple. Where you can distinguish your business is in persistent execution that gives life to your model.

- Resilience: Great business models must be resilient. Where possible, protect your model through proprietary rights.

- Room for improvements: A business model is like a living organism. It must evolve and grow through modifications and improvements.

Factors to consider in business modelling: The best business models are built around answering some important questions. The simplest modelling considerations are the ones proffered by the renowned academic, Professor Peter Drucker:

1. Who are your customers?

2. What does the customer value?

3. How would you deliver the value to your customer at an appropriate cost?

Other questions that would need to be answered will include: How can you create the value the customers require, that is, what will be the production and delivery processes? At what acceptable costs can value be created and delivered? What resources do you need to provide value? Who will be your key partners, such as suppliers, distributors, etc.? How will transactions be processed? How can you profitably keep ahead of the competition?

In addition, you will need to consider the following:

- Are your products novel? Or are they readily available from competitors, and if so, how will you offer them better?

- In deciding who your customers are, you have to be sure what they value in your product. Customers can, for instance, be sensitive to price, quality or after-sales service. Identify what your customers value and work to create how you could deliver that seamlessly and repeatedly. Although you must always have the end-users in mind, you may not always sell directly to them.

- Decide on the extent of vertical or horizontal integration, if any, in your supply chain.

- Decide on your business location: Depending on what you do, location can determine the success chances of your business. Hoteliers know that it is always about 'location, location and location'. Similarly, manufacturing businesses would always need to strike a wise balance between the need to be near the source of their raw materials or be close to their markets.

- How do you differentiate your product? Even for so-called 'commodities', you will need to differentiate your product to increase your chances of success in the market. Decide on key areas you can offer your product better than the competition. Depending on what your products are, who your end-users are, etc., you can differentiate your products through better pricing, better packaging, place utility, timing, better quality, aesthetics, performance, etc.

The schematic below is a simple representation of some of the factors to consider in building a business model.

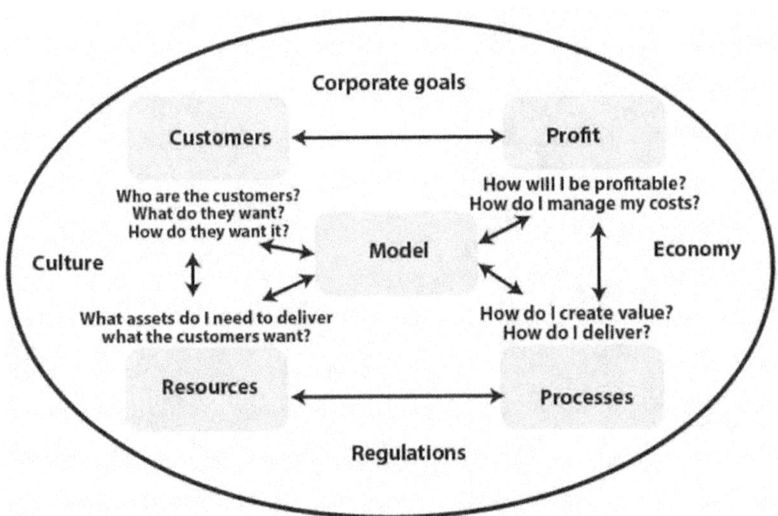

Figure 6.1: Business modelling factors
(© Musbahu El Yakub)

Business modelling is fundamental to business success. Ensure that you are deliberately thoughtful and innovative in creating a model that will provide value to your customers and keep you ahead of competitors profitably.

7.0 Planning Your Business

The survival and success of the human race over the last thousands of years are significantly attributable to our thinking capacity. Similarly, the survival, growth and eventual sustainable success of any business are largely attributable to the quality of the *thinking* and *actions* of the operators that guide and run it. We will now discuss the thinking component behind every successful business: business planning.

Business planning is the clear mental outlining of the premise and purpose of a business as well as the detailed strategies for achieving desired objectives. The final product of a business planning process is called a business plan. A business plan is, therefore, a usually written roadmap that brings out the philosophy behind a business as well the outline of the actionable strategies expected to achieve the objectives of the business through the use of resources.

Business plans are imperative for the success of an enterprise for several reasons.

Internal benefits of business plans: Within the organisation, the business planning process forces the entrepreneur and their team to think through the details of the business and its environment. This brings about a required understanding that is necessarily required if the business is to stand a reasonable chance of achieving success. Business plans also help in shaping policies that will remove ambiguity whenever actions are required to be taken. Eliminating ambiguity, even in the best thinking organisations, reduces waste and enhances a more efficient utilisation of resources.

External benefits of business plans: In the first instance, the quality of a business plan suggests to third parties the level of diligence and commitment of the entrepreneur and their team. Even more importantly, business plans are usually required by financiers and investors to assess any level of exposure they can take on the organisation. Business plans might also be required by government and non-governmental organisations that can provide grants and other support to a business.

Types of business plans: There are different types of business plans. First, there are *start-up business plans* that should be developed by start-ups to outline what the business will be about and how its objectives will be achieved. A *growth plan,* on the other hand, is a plan that is developed by a business that has achieved a certain level of success but wishes to achieve some specific growth objectives. A *functional plan* could also be drawn for a specific aspect of the business, such as marketing or finance. A functional plan should, however, be integrable and reconciled with other sub-components as well as the overall corporate plan. In fact, even if a business is to be wound down, a plan should be developed to do that deliberately, intelligently and at minimum costs.

Features of a business plan: A business plan should definitely be documented. But it doesn't have to be a thousand-page long. Depending on the size and scope of the business, a few pages can suffice. Regardless of its size though, a business plan must be comprehensive. It should cover all the appropriate aspects of the business and its environment. A business plan should be simple to read and understand and devoid of hyperboles and rigmaroles.

A business plan should be a stable, well-thought-out and action-biased document. And while circumstances could force a review at any time, the appropriate thing to do is to put in place a periodic reassessment system.

Elements of a business plan: A business plan covers every important aspect of a business conceptualisation and operation. Its elements are basically two: the environmental and the internal. The environmental elements will include economic and industry conditions, external opportunities and threats, etc. On the other hand, internal elements will include resources, such as human capital, available finances, functional strategies, etc. At the end, the plan will outline a general company description and how identified opportunities will be seized. The schematic diagram below depicts the dynamic interactions between resources and results built on a foundation of a business premise and philosophy and achieved through strategies within an operating environment.

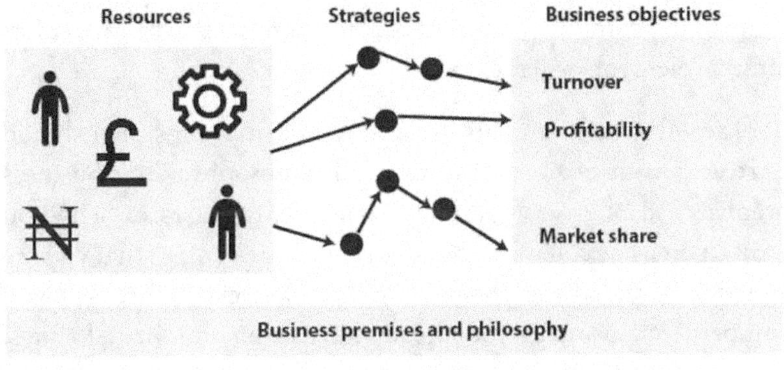

Figure 7.1: Business plan factors
(© Musbahu El Yakub)

Who should draw business plans? For many mature businesses, growth and even start-ups with sufficient resources, there is, often, the temptation to abdicate the responsibility of drawing business plans to external consultants. While there can be great value in involving them, it is necessary that the entrepreneur and their team participate fully in the process. Involvement in the process is key to bringing out and understanding the deep issues of the business as well as internalising them. Understanding and internalising the issues will help in building the mental preparedness of the entrepreneur as well as their capacity to take actions as may be required.

The Content of Business Plans

The first thing to understand is that, for our purposes here, the content of a business plan is different from its *presentation*. The content of a business plan remains generally the same, but the presentation and emphasis may differ from one business to another and from one recipient to another.

The best way to derive what the content of a business plan should be is from its 'elements' that we discussed. The internal elements, as we said, will include resources, such as human capital, available finances, functional strategies, competitive advantages, etc. So, some of the content of a business plan from the perspectives of its internal elements will include:

Business Premise and Philosophy: Your business plan should start with your business premise and philosophy. Your business premise and philosophy are the fundamental bases on why you want to do what you want to do or why you are doing what you are already doing. This might include internal factors, such as some competitive advantage you already have or environmental issues, such as opportunities in a market space. It may also be just your personal philosophy about something you hold dear or that you believe. Your reasons, whatever they are, must, however, be established to be commercially feasible.

Sam Walton started Walmart on simple principles. Those principles were also part of his strategies. They include the belief that people deserved to get quality goods at cheap prices. Similarly, Mr. Walton originally opened his stores in small and rural communities because he wanted to avoid competition and also believed that those communities deserved access to a large variety of goods at cheap prices. Opened first in 1962, Walmart had a turnover of $524 billion from some 11,500 stores and eCommerce websites in 2020.

About Your Company: Regardless of the specific purpose you may be developing your business plan for, you should know and write comprehensively about your company. These should include your company's legal status, the *raison d'etre* of its incorporation, those behind it as major shareholders, executives and management, product offering, what capabilities you have that distinguish you from your competition, etc.

Marketing Plan: Your marketing plan is to fully describe how you intend to serve your target market profitably. This should include what products you are or will be offering, your target market, logistics and, specifically, the delivery plans to your customers, service plans, etc. Your marketing strategy should bring out how you intend to do things differently and better than the competition in ways that will enable you to achieve your objectives.

Depending on the size and scope of your business, details about your competition, sales strategy, and promotions may be included here or composed separately. Irrespective of what you opt to do, the issues must be thoroughly discussed.

Financial Plan: Your business plan should include details about your financial resources and strategy. *What is your current financial situation? Do you have all the finances you require? If you have any financial needs, how do you intend to meet them? What are the current financial performances of the business? What is your credit policy?*

Your financial plan should also bring out what your financial targets and projections are as well as how you intend to achieve them. Your financial strategy should be discussed in detail. Issues like funding and liquidity management, relevant financial ratios, etc. should all be presented.

Human Resources: The most important resource of any organisation is its human capital. Irrespective of the size of your business, therefore, you should highlight the strength of your human capital. Bring out the experiences and qualifications of your key people as well as their past and current achievements. Where there are few key people, you will need detail on how the operations of the business are protected from any risks to them.

Operations: Depending on the nature/type and scope of your business, you will need to discuss your production and overall supply chain operations. These will include raw materials sourcing and processing, as well as delivery to your distributors or consumers. Any cost benefits that dovetail into your financial plan should be brought out. In our context, it is appropriate, for instance, to bring out how your perishable goods will be protected from risks whilst in transit on our roads.

Any modern or state-of-the-art technology that you have in your production plant, some Customer Relationship Management application that you have, etc., should be discussed here and the advantages they offer your business over and above the competition.

Attachments: If you are communicating your business plan to a third party, you may attach copies of incorporation documents, permits, property rights, patents, licences, contracts, some key staff resumes, etc. You may also include photographs of equipment, farmland, products, marketing materials, charts on financial and market status and projections, etc.

After the typical content of a business plan from the perspective of the internal elements of a business, the next set of variables shall be the content of a business plan from the perspectives of the environmental elements of a business.

The environmental elements of your business plan will include economic and industry conditions, external opportunities and threats, etc. Accordingly, some of the environmental elements of a business that should feature in a business plan will include the following:

Economic situation: The global meltdown of 2008, the Nigerian recession of 2016 and the COVID-19 pandemic of 2020 are real pointers on how economic, health and even political situations could impact negatively on businesses locally and internationally. Your industry and firm will operate within the overall context of the local and international communities. Your operations and success will be significantly impacted upon and to some extent, at least, determined by these two composite variables and your actions and responses to them.

A thorough economic analysis is to the business what a medical check-up is to the individual. It is aimed at bringing alive the awareness of the entrepreneur to the operating context of a business in its environment. Conditions such as technology, globalisation and labour supply as well as interest rates, commodity pricing and inflation will impact your operations. How will you preclude some and respond to others? How will the costs of inputs determine your business profitability and sustainability over time?

Industry analysis: An industry description is a comprehensive review and intelligent analysis of the industry within which your firm will operate. What are commercial attractions or disincentives to the industry? What are the barriers to entry and exit? Is it a growing or dying industry? What are the long-term and short-term commitments that a successful firm in the industry has to make? What are your personal opinions and philosophies about trends in the industry and how do they reconcile, or not, with professional projections?

Your company profile and its strategic positioning in the industry, over both space and time, should be discussed here and the specific actions you will take or are already taking to position your business in good stead in the industry.

Market analysis: At the end of everything, the aspiration of every business is a commercial success in the marketplace. Your market analysis should start with a very clear definition of the market you will be operating in: The full demographics and growth rate of the market; The spending power of your customers; How, specifically, will you attract and retain customers? What will be your pricing structure, distribution channels, etc.? What is the lifetime value of your customers? Which companies are market leaders and with what market shares? How will you gain, hold and grow market shares? Etc.

All the relevant statistics of the market as well as the firm-specific actions you will be taking should be brought out here to highlight your understanding of the market operations, its imperatives and your success strategies.

Competition: Customarily, your business will operate alongside other competitors. To stand good chances of success, you have to have a keen understanding of your competition, its mindset, beliefs, strengths and weaknesses. What is the cost structure of your competitors? How can you do things better than the competition? Which of your actions will distinguish you and put you ahead in the minds and pockets of customers?

In this part of your business plan, you are to demonstrate your knowledge and understanding of your competitors and how you can establish an edge and stay ahead of them.

Opportunities and Threats: There can be internal opportunities as well as threats to a business, arising, for instance, due to the ownership of intellectual property rights and staff incompetence, respectively. Similarly, there can be external threats and opportunities to a business. What are the current external opportunities your business is already enjoying? How can you position your business to seize emerging external opportunities? What are also the likely threats, arising from, say, new entrants and competitors, regulators or plain old environmental risks? The traditional SWOT analysis is crucial in bringing out, at least, limited realities of the operating environment. At the end, understanding opportunities, risks and threats is about the preparedness of the entrepreneur and the optimum positioning of a business to those realities.

Regulations: In any law-abiding human society, regulations by government agencies and even voluntary associations are a reality that affects what businesses may or may not be able to do. Certain industries and businesses are, by nature and quite understandably, more prone to government regulations. In whatever industry you may operate, you have to understand what regulations may apply to you and your business as well as their likely positive or negative impacts on your operations.

Your business plan should bring out applicable regulations and the likely impact they may have on your operations as well as your compliance levels and how you may legitimately seize them to your commercial advantage.

Business Plan Presentation

As mentioned earlier, the content of a business may remain the same but certain emphasis and indeed presentation may differ from one purpose to another. Regardless of the purpose though, the facts you present must stand any and every integrity check and test that the recipient might subject it to.

The presentation of a business will usually take the following standard format:

Title Page: The title page is simply the title page. It should capture the title of the plan and any caveats that are appropriate. If it is presented to a particular recipient and for a purpose, this should be clearly stated. The title page is usually not more than one page.

Executive Summary: An executive summary is a brief about the business plan. Key objectives, strategies and metrics are brought out here. Similarly, timelines for the objectives to be achieved are also mentioned. An executive summary should suffice on a page and certainly not more than two.

About Your Company: This is where you introduce and describe your company, its history, operations, etc. When was the company incorporated? What have you been doing? What are your experiences, failures and successes? What do you want to achieve? Etc. Depending on your business age, size and scope of operations, anything from two to five pages should suffice. In this section of the report, the reader should be made interested in what you are doing and what you want to do.

The Industry: Discuss the industry in which you are or will be operating. What are the difficulties and challenges in the industry? Who are the current big players? What are the big players doing differently? What is your company's current position in the industry and where do you want to be over what period of time?

Are there any government regulations peculiar to your industry? What are the industry trends and external influences?

The Market: Define the market you will be serving. What is the size of the market? What are the sales revenues of the major players in the industry? What are the physical locations of your customers? At what rate is the market growing? If the market is shrinking, why are you considering going into it? Is there a perfect match between the industry offering and market needs?

How will your company compete and stay ahead of the competition?

The Opportunity: What is the opportunity you want to seize? Are no other operators serving that need? How will you provide the goods or services required?

Your Strategy: You have earlier mentioned the market and opportunity you wish to serve. Now you will bring out the details of *how* you will serve the market. This will involve the deployment of all the resources, such as staffing, financial, knowledge, property rights, logistic advantages, etc.

Marketing Plan: A market plan is the core of your business plan. You are to bring out not just what part or parts of the market you wish to serve, but also the details of how you can profitably do that.

Operational Plan: Depending on your business, operations can be critical to success. This might be as *soft* as developing codes to *hard* production, distribution and delivery of pizza. What are your operational locations, including offices, warehouses and shops?

If there are any manufacturing processes, you should describe them here and how yours might be better and ahead of the competitors'.

Whatever your business operation, you have to bring out how it will serve customers' needs and be profitable to you.

Financial Plan: Any business idea, proposition or operation can easily get killed without the required finances. Your financial plan must show what your financing requirements are and how you will meet them on a continuous basis.

What is your cost structure? What are your revenue and cash projections? At what point will you breakeven and what will be your profit projections? Detailed financial projections of your cash flow, income statement and statement of affairs (balance sheet) over a reasonable number of years, typically five, should be made. The assumptions underlying the projections should be clearly stated.

Your Team: Truly and truly, the most important resource you can have are the people in your organisation. If you have the right and competent people, most issues can always be addressed. Describe your team members, their experiences, what value they add, etc.

What is the organisational structure? Who are the key executives and their roles?

Conclusion: Your conclusion should be a summary of what the plan has brought out. If there are any specific requests, such as some financial intervention, it is here you can restate them.

Appendices: Some charts and reports will be part of the write-up. Other relevant charts, reports, references, etc. should be added and attached at the end as appendices. Ensure that each appendix is appropriately titled and referred to in the main body.

Make your business plan beautiful, use the right fonts and sizes. Use colours where appropriate, etc.

8.0 Staffing

All organisations have various stakeholders. For a company, the stakeholders will include *investors* who provide the seed and risk capital required to commence and grow the business at various stages; the *employees* who run the daily affairs of the company; the *communities* in which the company operates; *creditors*, such as bankers that provide various types of funding; *government regulators*, such as NNRA and NAFDAC that have to provide some authorisations to a business operation, use of certain equipment or sale of products; the *customers* that buy your products; *suppliers* of your equipment, raw materials and other consumables, etc.

All the stakeholders play various and important roles in the operations of a business and the entrepreneur that will have any reasonable chance of succeeding must understand the roles, rights and responsibilities of each stakeholder group and how to manage those relationships.

Stakeholders such as investors and creditors may provide funds that are needed for the operations of a company; other stakeholders, such as suppliers, might supply raw materials of the right quality; customers may buy the products of a business, thereby providing required revenues to cover the costs of operations and generate profit. But central to all these dynamics are the employees of the business who interface with the financiers, suppliers, customers, regulators, etc.

Employee competence is necessary for success: It is employees that operate the machinery which produces the goods that the company sells. Any carelessness in machinery settings and your raw materials will be wasted, costs will increase and quality standards might not be met. Now, even if the manufacturing staff produce the right quality goods, it will take a motivated set of other personnel to market and sell the products to customers. After sales are made, credit control, accounts and audit officers will need to keep proper and accurate records that will provide management with relevant information for effective decision-making. Any weakness, at any point along the chain, will likely be multiplied and the compound effect undermines the chances of success.

Employee motivation determines their commitment and loyalty levels: The most successful companies in the world, such as Google, L'Oréal and Hilton, are known to have a highly motivated workforce. The level of motivation of these employees enhances their creativity levels, thereby making it easy for them to come up with solutions to otherwise daunting challenges.

It is employees that deploy and use all other resources: As mentioned earlier, investors, creditors, governments, etc. can all provide resources, such as finances, Enterprise Resource Planning applications, grants, concessions and licenses, but it will be your employees that can use those assets to deliver tangible results by adding value which customers will profitably pay for. Without competent and highly motivated employees, your company cannot deliver optimum and desired results regardless of all other resources committed to it.

The significance of employees in the success of a business is particularly critical in a developing economy like Nigeria's for at least a few more reasons:

High costs of operations: High costs of input, such as imported raw materials as well as energy and logistics, are generally exorbitant in Nigeria. Other difficult-to-predict-or-plan-for costs, such as unofficial levies and charges within cities and on our highways, all add to the already punitive costs of operations in our country. Incompetent and fraudulent staff increase these costs through more waste and collusion, thereby making your business utterly uncompetitive.

Wieldy and business-unfriendly government regulations: Small, medium and large businesses in Nigeria have to navigate a lot of less-than-friendly government regulations. From cumbersome registration procedures to the need for permits, signages, tax and pension payments, the Nigerian entrepreneur should have competent people that can ensure the effective navigation and compliance of the maze at minimum costs.

Access to capital and credit: At various points in the life cycle of the business, the entrepreneur will need to access more capital and credit for different purposes. There are now various vehicles and options for raising funds for a business. To succeed, the entrepreneur and their employees will need to understand the complexities of each option and also be able to meet the procedural, technical and behavioural requirements of raising money.

Poor staff attitude to work: One of the biggest challenges that Nigerian entrepreneurs face is a poor attitude to work by staff. Yes, whilst there is a percentage of hardworking, competent and trustworthy staff, there is, sadly, quite another large percentage of staff that isn't diligent and can be less-than-honest at the expense of the business. An entrepreneur ought to set the right standards in employing the right people, motivating and keeping them.

Risk assessment and management competencies: We have discussed elsewhere in the past the need for the entrepreneur to understand the risks that their business is exposed to and mitigate the same. Small and medium enterprises in Nigeria are exposed to risks on exchange rates, goods-in-transit, theft and pilferages, fire and natural hazards, etc. Having the right and competent people will help to understand the risks the business assumes at various points and times and also take appropriate actions to manage those risks.

Succeeding in business is about doing several things right. It is about avoiding many wrong things. It takes the right people with the right knowledge, skills, energy and attitude to succeed. So far, we have just tried to bring to the fore the importance of your employees in the scheme of your business and the reality that no matter how good your business proposition may be, competent, motivated and happy employees are a necessary condition for the ultimate survival, profitability and growth of your business. Next, we will look at the specific factors you should consider in recruiting employees for your budding business.

Business organisations are set up basically to meet some customer need, desire or expectation through value addition. This entails doing several things all at the same time consistently and persistently. To achieve these basic but fundamental objectives, you need the right people with certain qualities. These qualities include, in a composite but not any order, the following:

Energy and drive: I suspect that the physical laws of entropy do have an equivalent in our social lives. Probably, it is the so-called Murphy's law, which states that anything that can go wrong will tend to go wrong, unless we do something about it. The point is we must *do something* if we are to be able to achieve a preferred outcome. This means our businesses should have people that have the energy and drive to get things done. Sometimes, it is about seizing some opportunity while some other times it is all about fencing off problems that can jeopardise the survival or growth prospects of the business. No matter, your staff must be up and doing, at any time, without regard to personal preferences and conveniences.

Relevant technical skills: Whatever energy and drive your people may have, they will not be able to achieve desired results if they do not have relevant technical skills that may be required in your chosen field. If you are into software development, you have to have people that are skilled, versatile and happy coding day and night! If you are planning to set up a cattle ranch, you should have people who understand livestock feeding and management. In addition, your people must not only be versatile in current practices, but they should also be interested in global developments and new best methods in your field of business. Simply put, they must have a passion and bias for continuous learning.

Social skills: An otherwise highly productive environment can get toxic if the people do not have the requisite social skills necessary to smoothen the rough edges of working together and with others outside the organisation. Social skills involve working well with colleagues in healthy and productive ways as well as interfacing with other stakeholders, such as customers, financiers, etc. At the core of our individual and collective ability to deliver optimum results in a sustainable and healthy way are our attitude and social skills. In the long run, our attitudes and social skills take us so much farther than our technical skills and knowledge, which only take us so far so fast.

Knowledge: The hunger for individual personal development of the staff is important in their ability and capacity to continuously deliver top-notch and optimum results. The individual that has the penchant to learn from others, teach others, read and attend training programs, conferences, etc. stands a good chance of knowing what is happening not just in their industry but also in the local and global economy. You should look out for employees that are continuously learning. Equally importantly, the organisation should, over time, capture, internalise and share its overall build-up of knowledge and experiences.

Integrity: Multibillionaire and arguably one of the most successful investors in the last few hundred years, Mr. Warren Buffet, says about recruitment, *"We look for three things when we hire. We look for intelligence, we look for initiative and energy and we look for integrity."* He went on to caution, *"...if they don't have the latter, the first two will kill you, because if you are going to get someone without integrity, you want them lazy and dumb!"* Similarly, the late Jon Huntsman, Sr., who built his chemical company from nothing to a $12 billion enterprise, attributed integrity to success. He argued that the difference between the unsuccessful, the temporary successful and those who become and remain successful is character.

Integrity builds success for you in a small, consistent but assured way as long as you have the skills required in your field and the energy to sustain you on your journey. Unfortunately, both entrepreneurs and their employees in our environment have adopted fraud as a 'smart' way of 'creating wealth'. Nothing can be further from the truth and reality, as a lack of integrity can only bring temporary 'successes' at the great risk of losing everything. It is stupid, unwise and unsustainable.

Success and success attitudes, like failure and failure attitudes, are contagious amongst people in ways that are subtle yet deep and relentless. Consequently, you should be diligent and thorough in getting the right people with the right skills and attitude to populate your enterprise if you are to engender a pervasive can-do mindset and success attitude. Lazy and dishonest staff must be avoided at all costs. But getting the right people is only the first step towards building a successful enterprise. With the right selection and recruitment, the next big staff challenge you will face and must address will be about staff retention to maximise productivity and minimise disruptions and turnover.

Figure 8.1: The process of recruiting staff should be thorough
(Image credit: Gerd Altmann from Pixabay)

Retaining Your Great Employees

Staff 'turnover' refers to the rate at which employees exit an organisation. It is calculated by dividing the number of staff that exit the organisation over a period, usually a year, by the average number of total staff over that period. A 'high staff turnover' means a relatively large percentage of staff leave the organisation in proportion to the average number of employees. A 'low staff turnover' means the converse. Though a high staff turnover is often disliked, it must be seen within the context of the business, industry and economic situation. Generally speaking, companies that engage in executing irregular contracts, such as construction companies, and similarly seasonal businesses like farming, *tend* to have higher staff turnover than those in, say, stable manufacturing industries.

Within the context mentioned, a high staff turnover is disliked for at least a few reasons: It is a costly and time-consuming process to recruit good employees; You lose time and expertise when your staff leave and before you successfully replace them; Even when you succeed in getting a good replacement, it will usually take some time before they fully settle into your system for their maximum productivity, etc. So, how do you retain the good staff you have recruited?

Pay them fairly and reasonably well: At different career points of employees, the same things mean different things. At some stage, usually the beginning, financial package is all that may be important and desired. At other stages, usually at middle and senior levels, job factors and non-financial benefits can become a lot more material. It is essential that you are cognisant of what will make the staff happy at which point in time and even location of their career.

Create an amiable environment: Various studies confirm that amiable environments enhance productivity. The most productive organisations are known to have amiable environments that are employee-friendly by being conducive, positive, supportive, etc. A Taiwanese business I interacted with has a large 'Quiet Room' in their exciting office where employees can go to rest, take a nap, freshen up and resume work!

Provide them with resources required to do their jobs well: One of the reasons many employees leave is because the organisations they work for do not provide them with the basic tools and other resources they require to work with. It is the responsibility of the entrepreneur and their executives to ensure that required resources are provided to employees.

Communicate and encourage employees to speak their minds: Poor or no communication can destroy an organisation regardless of the resources made available to staff. You should put in place a system of clear and honest communication and also encourage your people to speak up and communicate with others.

Reward performance: It is important that you have a fair and transparent system of rewarding high performance. High performers have, understandably, a desire for financial and non-financial rewards and recognition. Besides, people do what you reward. If you, therefore, want high performance, you must reward it in ways your staff will be happy with.

Don't punish innocent failures: The most successful people and organisations are always doing so many things. Thus, it is no surprise that they also often 'fail'. Interestingly, if they were to target zero failure as an objective, they are very likely to be a lot less successful. Consequently, you have to allow room for innocent and good-faith failures in your organisation. You just should have systems to support your people in what they are trying to do and be quick and responsive to managing the consequences of occasional failures without demotivating the employees involved. Have the good sense to laugh at some failures and learn from them.

Respect people: Even animals maintain social hierarchies and respect is often enforced in clans. Creating an environment in which there is mutual respect amongst employees regardless of position and status will go a long way in enhancing productivity through building the amiable environment we mentioned earlier.

Don't micromanage: It is funny, if not pathetic, how entrepreneurs and executives recruit good staff and yet micromanage them. If you are looking for the top initiative-killer, look no further. Your best and confident employees will leave you sooner than later if you micromanage them. Giving free hands to staff within their areas of responsibilities engenders trust and confidence and is the fastest way of developing your staff for higher duties.

Train and develop your people: The world in general and the economic and business environments, in particular, are continuously changing. Just think how rapidly the COVID-19 pandemic altered the global business landscape within a few weeks. The only way your organisation can adapt and grow at the same time is if your employees are continuously developing themselves. In-housing mentoring, lectures, experience and knowledge-sharing as well as external training, attending industry exhibitions and business conferences, etc., are all ways that your staff should be availed to keep themselves abreast of developments.

Fire them fairly! Unfortunately, there are times when entrepreneurs must discharge some staff. Perhaps, it is due to some wrongdoing or incompetence. It could also be due to a downturn in the economy which necessitates some cost-cutting measures. Whatever might be the reason for disengaging your staff, you should ensure that you do it properly and fairly. Do not shirk away from any of your responsibilities.

Just recently, I was involved with a company whose Chief Executive was leaving. Unfortunately, some members of the Board of Directors were legalistic in their demands on the disengagement process. Whilst that may be right, I took a different position and strongly suggested that discussions should be held so that some amicable settlement that is acceptable to both parties could be reached. I think it is always good to try to part on a good note. Truly the world is so much smaller than we ever think.

9.0 Funding Your Business

Funds are critical to business success and raising them can be daunting. But raising funds is part of the puzzle pieces that must be continuously put in place if any entrepreneurial masterpiece is to be created. In business history, limited or even complete lack of funds has only brought out the best of the creative minds and resourcefulness of great entrepreneurs. The individual that does not make any effort to start a business because they think or believe it will be difficult or impossible to raise the required capital display nothing but their weak motivation and lack of sufficient appetite for going into entrepreneurship.

When Ross Perot left IBM as a salesman to start EDS in 1962, all he had in savings for the business was $4,000.00. The amount was so insufficient that they could not afford to fix a door to the office restroom. They made do with a flimsy curtain instead! Twenty-two years later in 1984, Ross Perot sold EDS to General Motors for $2.5 billion! There are several unrecorded but known similar success stories, even if for different magnitudes, in Nigeria and Africa. Tight funds for start-ups are known to engender creativity and resourcefulness in a budding enterprise whilst excess funds over reasonable estimates of requirements can cause wastefulness and lethargy both of which are dangerous to the efficiency and overall grit of the business DNA.

Having said that, we know that funds are the lubricants that keep the moving parts of an enterprise going. Raising funds could be easy or challenging depending on several factors, such as the individual entrepreneurs' situation, the quality of the business proposition and other environmental factors. But before we discuss funding options and structures, we need to first understand the broad purposes for which funds may be required in a business. This is crucial because the *utilisation* to which funds will be put should determine the source, form and structure of the funds to be taken. Some of the purposes are as follows:

Pre-business take-off: Before your business takes off, you will need to conduct feasibility tests involving studies that you could either handle or may have to engage and pay professionals for. After the studies, you will need to draw up your business plan, do some pilot tests, etc. You will also need to register your proposed business name with the appropriate regulators. After registration, you may need certain approvals-in-principle, permits and/or licences. You may also have to employ some key and initial staff that you need even before you commence production. All these will cost you money and they are called **pre-operational expenses**.

Business take-off: For your business to take off, you may need to have an office and/or factory space and equipment, such as those for production as well as for office administration and logistics; you may also need raw materials and funds for salaries, utilities, marketing, etc. These imply that in addition to covering preoperational expenses, you will also need funds to acquire **fixed assets** as well as **current assets**.

Fixed assets refer to assets with more than a one-year expected life that are used in the production of goods as well as in providing auxiliary services. These may include real estate, factory equipment that may be expected to last some fifteen years; motor vehicles that may be depreciated over a period of four years and indeed even light assets like office desktop computers that may be written off after some two or three years. On the other hand, your current assets are those that facilitate the day-to-day business operations and are readily convertible into cash within one year. Current assets will include cash, prepaid expenses, accounts receivables, raw materials, etc.

Growth: One of the fundamental goals of all successful entrepreneurs is the continued growth of their businesses. Growth could mean more production output, which would require more equipment capacity and more raw materials, with consequential increase in staff salaries and the costs of logistics. As opportunities open up, business growth will be a permanent moving target in an enterprise. Planning for funding growth is vital to every expansion plan and seizing unforeseen opportunities. The successful entrepreneur must be deliberate and wise about planning for growth funds.

Management of Statement of Financial Affairs: Sometimes it may be expedient or in the interest of a business to restructure its balance sheet. Common issues in this regard are the consolidation or refinancing of debt. Funds could be raised to restructure existing debts to reduce cost and debt management complications or for other legitimate strategic objectives.

It should be noted that the type of funding required to purchase factory equipment that will last twenty years can be markedly different from the type of funds that will be required for the purchase of raw materials to be used in production and sold within sixty days. For each of the broad requirements above, therefore, the entrepreneur should identify the specific financial needs of the business on an immediate basis as well as a reasonable projection into the future. With this information on hand, the entrepreneur will then begin to identify specific possible source(s) and the structure of funding for each purpose.

Funding Structure

So far, we have introduced the various *uses* to which funds are put to in a business. We made it importantly clear that the use to which funds will be put must have a bearing to the *type* of finance as well as its *source*. Let's assume you need twenty million Naira for a minor capacity expansion program. Let's also say that out of the said amount, ten million Naira is needed to purchase an equipment that will last for ten years and the other ten million Naira will be used to procure more raw materials that will be processed into final products to be sold in cycles of three months each. So, even though the two amounts are the same, but because the purposes (read: *uses*) are different and, consequently, the *'recovery rates'* of the funds will also be different, then the *type* of finance for each *use* should be different.

Generally speaking, there are two types of funds: **Equity** and **Debt**.

Equity financing: At the point you start, you may own one hundred per cent of your business. However, if you want to inject more capital into the business, you can 'sell' a certain percentage of it to investor(s) by offering 'shares' at an agreed price. Individuals and organisations can invest in your company if you can convince them of the proposition and the possible benefits accruable to them. By buying shares, the investors become equity holders in and part-owners of your company.

More often than not, equity investors would provide cash for the shares sold to them. But it is also possible for investors to provide other assets, such as real estate, raw materials, equipment, etc. in return for the agreed stake.

There are at least a few types of equity investments that can be made. Irrespective of its type, equity financing is generally long-term and its owners are not paid interest or other obligations as may be paid to lenders. Equity financing, therefore, places the least financial burden on an organisation but is riskier than debt from the investors' perspective. For instance, in the event that the business has to be wound up for whatever reason, the owners of the equity will be the last to be paid after creditors and other liabilities are settled. Notwithstanding, equity owners expect performance and reasonable returns on their investment through dividend pay-out as well as capital growth over time.

Debt financing, on the other hand, means an external source, such as a bank lending you money with an obligation on your part to pay back the amount at an agreed interest rate and time period.

There are different types of debts. Some are interest-bearing whilst others are not or may only be interest-bearing on certain conditions. A bank loan is a straight interest-bearing debt. But with developments in non-interesting bearing financing models, institutions now also lend to fund transactions on 'profit-sharing' basis. Regardless, neither ownership stake nor control is surrendered by the business owner(s) to the lender. However, lenders can insist on taking a charge on some assets of the business and may also put in conditions and restrictions on the activities the business may do or how it may do it.

Other liabilities that help run your business include trade credit in which suppliers of raw materials may give you goods on credit and you are to make payment at a pre-agreed price at some time in the future. Some trade suppliers will put in an interest clause such that, if you fail to pay within the agreed period, you will begin to pay interest at a rate on the amount outstanding.

Prudent and pragmatic use of debt can help to create more wealth by making it possible for a company to seize opportunities that would otherwise be passed. If your business hits hard times or doesn't grow as fast as expected, however, debt can become really burdensome on the operations of a company. Furthermore, if you fail to pay your debt, your lender can foreclose on not just your business assets pledged but also your personal assets if you have given your personal guarantee for the loans extended.

Debt-Equity mix: In real life, most businesses have a mix of debt and equity financing. As the owner of the business, you need to be alert to your business gearing and your debt-equity ratios. Your business gearing refers to the amount of loans funding your business. If you have too much debt, you are said to be highly geared. If you have too much debt in comparison to the equity in the business, you are said to have a high debt-equity ratio. Lenders will always look out for your gearing and debt-equity ratios whenever they are considering giving you a loan you applied for. An optimum mix of debt-equity combination is what you have to strive continuously to maintain. Different industries tend to have different gearing levels and debt-equity mixes. Regardless though, an entrepreneur must be alert to their debt-equity dynamics and the implications it has on business risks, results and reputation.

Funding Sources

For our purposes, we can simply classify funding sources into the *Informal* and the *Formal*.

Informal sources: These are sources of funds at which not much rigorous review of your business proposition or financing request is conducted. Usually, such sources tend to just be compassionate and even indulgent about the support they are providing to the entrepreneur as a person. Informal sources provide the entrepreneur with loans at concessionary or no interest at all as well as outright equity investment without much expectations, demands, conditions or even a legal intent. Other than the entrepreneur themselves, other informal sources of loans and investments are friends, family, professional colleagues, crowdfunding, etc.

Informal sources are great at helping to kick-start your business as they can, usually, provide funds timely and without preconditions. Similarly, informal sources can help to finance the limited expansion and growth of a budding business. Little documentation, if any, is done when funds are made available from these sources.

Inherent in the advantages of informal loans and investments are also its disadvantages. First, informal sources usually do not have much discretionary loanable and/or investible funds to meet the large financing requirements of the entrepreneur. Secondly, the business is not subject to dispassionate reviews that can help to strengthen it and eliminate or minimise avoidable wastages. Even worse than all that, if the entrepreneur does not do the right things in running the business very well and paying back the loans/recouping the investments, key life relationships can be strained.

To make a success of funding from informal sources, the entrepreneur should commit reasonable and verifiable personal resources to the business to demonstrate their confidence in the proposition. The entrepreneur should also understand and respect that people are trusting them with their life savings and investments, which must not be taken lightly. Consequently, the entrepreneur should be diligent and forthright not just in doing their best but in also providing regular details to the creditors and investors. Equally importantly, documentation should be done properly and in necessary detail to keep records of terms, agreements and any expected performances.

Formal sources: This refers to those sources of funds at which your business proposition and your funds' requisition are subjected to thorough reviews, analysis, tests and processing for ultimate approval or rejection. Furthermore, formal sources will, rightly, always and unambiguously seek to create legal relations with the entrepreneur and the business. But while informal sources usually have limit to the amounts they can loan to or invest in you, formal sources are literally a boundless barn of financial resources.

In addition to loans and equity investments, formal sources of funds can also provide the entrepreneur with informed business intelligence and advisory that can help to strengthen their business model and enhance operational efficiency and profitability. For the loans provided to your business, formal sources will often ask for collateral to secure their exposure to you; they will charge interest as well as arrangement/management fees, default penalties, etc.; For equity investments, these sources will demand for a percentage shareholding of the business and perhaps some Board seat(s) and even certain executive management positions as well.

One of the big mistakes that budding entrepreneurs often make at the beginning or some other growth stage of their business is to be obsessed with their shareholding stake. Obviously, the more percentage you can retain the more control you may continue to have on your business and also the likely financial returns. But the timeless advice of the late Chief Gamaliel Onosode on this issue is for the entrepreneur to understand that a small percentage ownership of a great business can be so much more valuable and beneficial than a large percentage ownership of a not-so-great business.

Depending on whether you are taking in equity investment or a loan, there may be different sources available to you. Private and public formal loan sources in Nigeria will include microfinance banks, commercial banks, government development finance institutions like the Bank of Agriculture, Bank of Industry, Nigeria Export-Import Bank, etc. The Central Bank of Nigeria provides massive direct and indirect financial support to businesses in Nigeria. We also have private and public sector agencies, incubators and accelerators that provide financial and non-financial support to entrepreneurs. These include the National Directorate of Employment, Small and Medium Enterprises Development Agency of Nigeria, the Nigeria Incentive-Based Risk Sharing System for Agricultural Lending plc., etc. Formal sources of equity investment include 'Angels' and Venture Capitalists. Leasing companies provide finance and operating leases, which can help to make available equipment to your business.

So far, we have tried to understand the usage of funds for business, the types of funds available to the entrepreneur for business and the sources of funds for a business. However, different sources of different funds have different requirements and processes for granting a loan or making an investment. For the informal loan and credit sources, their requirements, as mentioned earlier, are usually simple, fairly fast and fluid. On the other hand, formal investment and loan sources have processes and standards that can take a life of their own!

Before going into loan requirements, processes and borrowing etiquettes, let us just say a word or two about formal investor requirements. Equity investors will normally look out for the quality of your business proposition. The quality of your proposition refers to its reality, strength and potential of building a sustainable and profitable customer base: *Are the business objectives already being achieved? If not, can they be achieved? Is the business scalable? What are the cash and profit positions of the business?* Etc. 'Risk-averse' investors look to a business that is already stable and with a lot of room for growth. Such investors might, for instance, invest in a foods and beverages business or real estate. Other investors with greater appetite for risk, like Venture Capitalists, look to innovative and disruptive businesses. These investors might be excited about investing in a firm introducing a new drug for the cure of Alzheimer's or some breakthrough in cloud technology. After the 'soundness' of a proposition, other factors that risk-averse investors would consider will be a *historical* record of solid profitability and cash flow. Our more 'risk-inclined' investors, on the other hand, will look out for the *prospects* of strong cash flow and profitability that can be achieved by a competent management on a proposition that has not been tested.

Loan Requirements, Processes and Borrowing Etiquettes

Loan requirements: Formal loan sources, such as banks, would always have a lending policy. It is the framework around which all the lending activities of the institution are built. Lending policies will cover issues like which industries to lend to; what minimum and maximum loan amounts can be granted; what types of collateral can be accepted from borrowers; what loan tenors can be accommodated; Will start-ups be funded or not, etc.

Consequently, the first thing the entrepreneur should do when they make contact with a lender is to find out if their loan request will fit into the lending sphere of the institution. If it wouldn't, don't waste your time unless you are sure there is sufficient basis that might interest the institution to consider you as an exception. However, if you establish that the lending policy will accommodate your request, you can begin to discuss what the requirements of the institution will be as regards your request. The officers will inform you what application documents and information will be expected from you; what collateral will be required; what the interest rate and other charges will be, etc.

Loan processes: Loan processing will involve the active engagement of the two parties. These engagements will be about the lending institution understanding your business and request and for you to understand what the loan requirements and process will be. Once sufficient mutual understanding is achieved, you can then submit your application with relevant documents, such as a feasibility report, business plan, audited/management accounts, cash flow statements or others, as may be required by the lender.

With all documents submitted, the lender will review your request. An officer or team will remain in touch with you, often asking for clarifications or additional documents. It is imperative that you are steadfast, diligent and forthright in providing any information. The institution will assess your request from general and specific perspectives. Some of the assessment criteria will be your character, business capacity, what collateral might be accepted, economic conditions, etc.

Different lending institutions have different response time frames. Depending on the loan, processing an application might end at a branch, regional or head office level. Once approval is granted to your request, an 'offer letter' stating the terms and conditions of the facility will be made out to you. It is necessitous that you review the offer letter with your legal advisor and financial consultants to understand every bit of it. If there are any difficult issues, you can raise them up at this time. Do not accept an offer whose terms or conditions, legal or financial, you cannot meet.

Borrowing etiquettes: As with all other aspects of your business, the moment you make the decision to borrow, you have to maintain an impeccable level of integrity in everything you say and do. All information and documents you provide to the lender must stand any integrity tests they may be subjected to. Similarly, do not commit to what you know you do not intend or will be impossible for you to deliver. Lenders would rather have terms reviewed on mutual agreement than for you to begin to falter and fail on the commitments you have pre-agreed to.

The best approach to relating with a lending institution is to take them on as 'partners' rather than 'adversaries' which many entrepreneurs are wrongly wont to do. With the right mindset, your approach to dealing with them will be that of good faith and well-meaning. You must have an unflinching commitment and resolve to service and pay your loans. Remain in regular contact with your lender and provide timely and relevant information. When things go wrong, as they often do, you should immediately communicate with your lender. If you need some loan restructuring, discuss it. If you are already handling the situation in your ways, let them know. If you need time to sort things out, let the lender know as well.

Chapter 3

"We are what we repeatedly do. Excellence, then, is not an act, but a habit."
- Will Durant

10.0 Record Keeping and Documentation

Some years ago, a company I was associated with was contacted by a 'Debt Collector' on the grounds that they were appointed by a bank to collect what the bank alleged as unpaid loan that the company took from the bank some twelve years earlier. We listened to but advised the Debt Collector that the bank needed to write to us about the appointment before we could respond to them in respect of the allegation, which was into several millions of Naira!

In under fifteen minutes of the receipt of the bank's letter appointing the Debt Collector, we were able to retrieve our documents evidencing full repayment of the loan. The documents included our duly acknowledged letter to the bank instructing them to sell the shares we borrowed the money to buy; the bank's own statement of account evidencing that the shares were sold by the bank on our instruction and the proceeds paid into our account, leaving us with a neat profit as the shares were sold at a price above the cost at which they were bought and the financial costs of the transaction. We wrote to the bank, attaching the undisputable documentary pieces of evidence of the repayment and the matter was fully rested without a whimper. Our twelve-year-old incontrovertible records and documents had saved us a lot of headaches.

Keeping records and documents, an important way of life and business is, unfortunately, not a culture we have fully adopted in our environment yet. Transactions and contracts are carried out without proper documentation and records are not necessarily kept well either. Any dispute becomes protracted and can be costly to all parties. But all that can be avoided.

What is record keeping and documentation? Record keeping is the process of building detailed, complete, accurate and reliable information on business transactions. On the other hand, documentation refers to the preservation of records in various formats. Whilst the two terms may be distinct, they are often used interchangeably.

The Benefits of record keeping and documentation:

- **Regulatory Compliance:** Keeping certain documents is required by law. Compliance documents, like business registrations, approvals to operate in certain industries and/or equipment, such as those that emit ionising radiations, etc., are all required by law. Keeping these records helps to keep you on the right side of the law.

- **Development of plans and strategies:** The information you keep about and for your business is a source of operational intelligence for you. They will reveal your strengths and weaknesses and be handy for the development of your plans and strategies, thereby helping to position you appropriately in the market.

- **Enhances corporate governance and creates opportunities:** Keeping records and documents enables you to engage positively with potential investors, financiers, suppliers, etc. who may consider doing business with you.

- **Eliminates ambiguities and protects your business:** Keeping records eliminates ambiguities and protects you and your business in disputes and from wrongful claims and counterclaims both of which will help you save time and money.

- **Establishes your credibility:** The first evidence of your and your business' credibility is the records and documents you keep as well as their quality and integrity. Keeping true and reliable records and documents is indicative of your transparency and credibility.

What types of records should you keep? The types of records you are to keep would depend on your business, scale, model, regulatory requirements, etc. Some of the records and documents that you must keep will include:

- **Registration documents:** I always strongly advise and encourage entrepreneurs to register their businesses and keep such records safe. Your registration documents are what give you the first legitimacy to operate as a business with certain corporate rights and responsibilities.

- **Operational transactions and communications:** All relevant activities of your operations should be recorded. Transactions and communications on all aspects of your operations should be captured and documented.

- **Financial documentation:** Specifically, you will need to keep financial records of transactions. Your financial records, like all others, will need to be kept both for your internal use as well for the use of regulators and potential business partners.

- **Contractual documents:** Certain documents, such as employee contracts, non-disclosure and non-compete agreements, loan offers, etc. must be kept for records as may be required for several legitimate reasons.

How do you keep records and documents? Records and documents can be kept in several ways and formats. But whatever system you use, make sure that all details are captured easily and seamlessly. You should also ensure that they meet your legal and operating requirements.

- **Time statute:** Records should be kept for a minimum of the period required by law. Preferably, you should keep them longer than that. With modern IT systems available now, keeping records for long should not be much of a challenge.

- **Control and retrieval:** Any recording system you have should allow for easy retrieval. It must also ensure security and control, meaning that only people with appropriate authorisations can access and use the information available. Document trails should be in place as well.

- **Security:** Records and documents should have backups and be kept safely and protected against sabotage and hazards.

To make sure that your business keeps records and documents appropriately and meticulously, you have to do three things simultaneously:

- **Train your people:** You have to train your people in the art and science of keeping records. Discussions and agreements internally and with external parties must be recorded as much as is required. Your people ought to be proficient in and comfortable with keeping records.

- **Don't take any chances:** A key aspect of the human side of record keeping and documentation is that your people should learn to be dispassionate and not take anything for granted.

- **Provide the required resources:** Records are kept in various ways. Ensure that your staff have the facilities they require to build and keep records and documents.

This gives us a snapshot of what record keeping and documentation are, their importance and how we can keep them.

11.0 Business Metrics

'What is measured improves.'
- Peter Drucker

'Strategy' and 'Execution' are two variables crucial to business success. But you cannot develop an effective strategy and efficiently get things done if you are not clear about the factors that drive performance and the variables that measure results. The measures of the drivers of business performance and results are what are known as business metrics, and it shall be our subject in the next pages.

After the Second World War, the Japanese needed to rebuild their country from the ruins of war. Key to the effort was to be the resuscitation of their industries. With the traditional obsession of the Japanese with quality, their focus was, unsurprisingly, on the quality of manufactured products. The idea was basically to ensure that the variation in the quality of products was reduced. Consequently, a statistical approach to quality control was used to improve the understanding and use of quality metrics. Over time, other processes were developed which led to the transformation of the orientation, focus, and even strategies of firms, supply chains and industries. Japan, raising from the ashes of war, led the globalisation of metric-driven success. Decades on, the world has come to accept Japanese products as being synonymous with quality which has continued to create traction for their businesses.

What are business metrics? Business metrics are quantifiable measures that a business uses to predict, track, monitor, assess and control the extent or success or failure of various business activities, processes, and overall performance. Business metrics, sometimes called Key Performance Indicators, 'KPIs', are often desired end results but also the direct and indirect bridges between efforts and the results.

Benefits of understanding and use of business metrics: The first major benefit of the use of metrics is the clarification of strategic objectives and operational goals. Irrespective of your business type, understanding what your key performance drivers are and using them appropriately to guide your people and business will make you efficient in the use of resources as well as effective in delivering results. These will in turn improve your service delivery, customer attraction and retention, and overall profitability. Specifically, your metrics can help you identify areas of operational and strategic successes as well as challenges and failures at individual, unit or corporate levels. Success can then be improved upon whilst failures and problems can be addressed.

Tracking the right business metrics will help you assess your performance over time or against a competitor or industry averages. Tracking your metrics will also allow you to be regulatory-compliant, clarify communications between units, strengthen business intelligence capacity, reduce transaction costs, etc.

Types of business metrics: There are literally hundreds of different metrics applicable across different business units, functions, processes, and industries. Even within the same organisation, different departments may use different metrics to monitor their local performances. For instance, manufacturing will have different metrics from sales and marketing which will also have different metrics from logistics. Accordingly, appropriate metrics will be determined by business type, corporate objectives, level of authority of official(s), functional responsibility and its scope, business process, etc. For our purposes here, however, we will be looking at possible metrics for the chief executive at a corporate level.

A simple schematic below shows some of the factors that influence the choice of corporate business metrics and how they get built up from different functions.

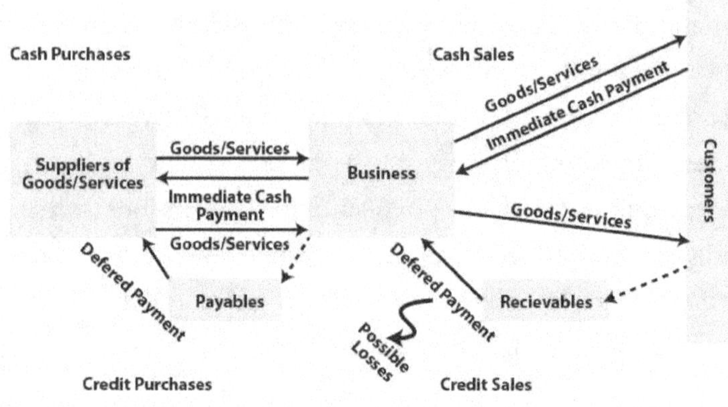

Figure 11.1: Corporate metrics and the factors that determine them
(© Musbahu El Yakub)

What business metrics should you use? Whilst there are textbook metrics that tend to be universal, you can, in fact, come up with a metric or metrics that may be peculiar to your business or situation. What is important is that your invented metrics should reliably predict and track desired performances.

Some metrics measure overall corporate, marketing and sales performances while others may measure financial, human capital or logistics performance. Key financial metrics that will provide insights into the operational efficiency of a business may include earnings before interest and taxes, net income, margins, rates of return, etc. It is also crucial to monitor liquidity and leverage ratios, etc.

Marketing metrics may include qualified leads, annual recurring revenues, cost per acquisition, cost per lead, customer lifetime value, etc. Production metrics might include manufacturing cycle time, throughput, overall equipment effectiveness, etc. Human resource management metrics might include staff turnover, *early* turnover rates, time since last promotion, revenue per employee,

employee happiness, etc. Social media metrics, if appropriate for your business, might include account reach, followers, post engagement rates, etc.

Characteristics of effective business metrics: To select the appropriate metrics for your people, functions and business, you have to look out for features such as:

- **Strategic** – Your chosen metrics should be strategic both in terms of being linked to corporate objectives as well as 'seeing' into the future.

- **Actionable** - Metrics must be actionable, meaning that your people ought to know what to do and be able to improve results by taking certain action(s).

- **Standardised** – Metrics should be standardised within an organisation by agreeing on their definitions and how they will be computed.

- **Accuracy** – Your systems must be reliable enough to ensure that metrics are obtained from reliable computations.

- **Aligned** – Metrics should be aligned within an organisation to avoid confusion, conflicts, and avoidable turf wars.

- **Relevance** – It is important to review metrics regularly to ensure that they remain relevant. Metrics can be dropped or adopted due to legitimate changes in goals, operations, or the environment.

An understanding of business metrics makes it easy for you to apply effort and other resources in achieving results.

12.0 Cash Flow Management

Business success is about doing several things right. We talked about creating value first, which must be desired by your target customers that will be willing to pay you for it at a profitable price. Beyond creating value at a selling price that is profitable, sustainable business success is about asset growth built from profits that is cash-backed. We will now take up cash flow management.

One of the principles of modern accounting is the concept of 'accrual'. This accrual principle requires that financial transactions are recorded in the time period in which they occur, regardless of when cash for the transaction is received in or paid out. The objective is to match revenues against expenses when transactions take place rather than when the payment for the transaction actually occurs. Whilst the accrual principle does help us in understanding the financial status of a business at any point in time, it does not show us what the actual cash position of the business is. This means that a business could show profits in its books but can go bankrupt for lack of cash! Consequently, it is crucial to understand what cash flow, its management and its importance are.

Cash flow cycle: Cash flows through a business in reasonably predictable ways. We either get supplies and services on credit or we pay for them in cash (which includes payments through your bank accounts). Similarly, we also sell our products (goods and services) either on credit or cash (which also includes payments made through your bank accounts). How we manage the receipts for our sales and make payments for the goods and services we purchase determines our cash conversion cycles and our net cash position at any point in time.

The common example given to explain your cash flow and cash position is to imagine a bathtub into which you can let water and out of which you can drain water, with the net water level representing your net 'cash position' at any point in time. The more water (i.e. cash) you want in the tub, the more you have to let in water from the tap (i.e. more cash collections from sales, investors, creditors, etc.) but at the same time you have to slow the drain (i.e. by delaying payments to suppliers of goods and service). *A note of caution at this point, however, is that no matter what you do to slow down cash outflow, you must always meet agreed payment terms with your suppliers. If, for unexpected legitimate reasons, you are unlikely to meet the terms, which should be an exception, you should negotiate and agree to new terms. Your credit reputation with suppliers is crucial to your success. More of this will be discussed later in this series.*

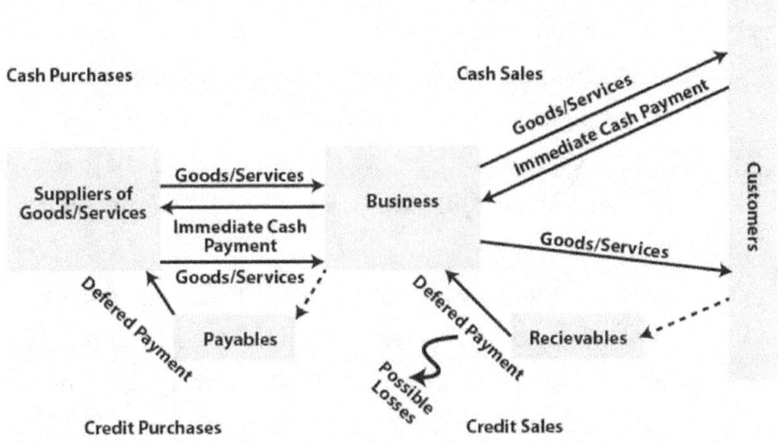

Figure 12.1: Basic cash flow dynamics
(© Musbahu El Yakub)

Understanding the cash flow cycle means you should understand the cash conversion process comprising working capital and even capital investment management. Assuming your capital investment decisions have been wise, prudent and optimum, you must be excellent at managing your working capital by understanding the impact of your inventory, receivables and payables on your cash position on a dynamic basis.

Key terms: You need to understand what basic working capital terms are:

- Liquidity refers to the ease with which an asset can be converted into cash without affecting its market value negatively. To be 'liquid' means to have cash and near cash assets that you can always draw on to settle obligations as they fall due and also seize opportunities.

- Cash and Bank balances refer to the cash holding you have in the office till or vault as well as in your bank accounts at any point in time. Generally speaking, this is the most liquid of all your assets.

- Account receivables are the debts owed to your business by your customers who have been *supplied* goods and services but have not yet made payment to you. (Note that this is regardless of whether the goods and services have been *used* by customers or not, unless there are terms to the contrary.)

- Inventory comprises various groups of materials and other consumables that are used to produce goods and services. This includes raw materials, work-in-progress, finished goods and some other consumables (so-called 'maintenance, repair and operating supplies'). Typically, your inventory ends up as final merchandise available for sales to your customers.

- 'Other current assets': Essentially, your cash/bank, receivables and inventory make up most of your 'current assets'. But apart from these three major categories, there may be other 'current assets' that your business could hold, such as marketable securities, prepayments, etc. The sum of all such assets forms what is called your current assets.

- Account payables are the short-term obligations due to your suppliers and other such creditors. If your raw material supplier provides you with goods for which payment will be made at a later date, you have a *trade payable* that will be due at the agreed future date.

- Current liabilities are your short-term financial obligations that will be maturing within a year or normal operating circle. Aside from your account payables, other current liabilities include accrued expenses, taxes payable, short-term debt, etc.

Your net working capital refers to the sum of all your current assets less the sum of all your current liabilities. Whilst different current assets and different current liabilities impact your liquidity position differently, it is necessary that you understand what each means and how each impacts on your operations. Actually, beyond understanding current assets and liabilities for cash management purposes, you also have to be fully conversant with financial statements comprising income statement and statement of financial position.

The Importance, Principles and Practices of Cash Flow Management

One of the issues I find both leery and amusing is that formal business schools will almost always teach and encourage entrepreneurs and businesses to keep minimum cash levels. It is generally rationalised, even mathematically proven, that cash is a low-earning asset. (In fairness, the schools also teach about the need to hold cash for reasons that are similarly discussed). I think the arguments for holding cash, depending on details, are, generally speaking, superior to that of not keeping cash. You see this in the actual practices of the biggest and most successful companies in the world.

Samsung Electronics of South Korea had a cash holding of about US$30 billion in December 2021 in addition to short-term investments of US$65.8 billion. Apple Inc. of the United States had a cash holding of US$26.9 billion in September 2021 in addition to US$35 billion in short-term investments. Berkshire Hathaway of the United States had a cash holding of US$88 billion in December 2021 in addition to US$58.5 billion in short-term investments. These are massive cash holdings that can be drawn from at any point in time to solve problems or seize opportunities. We have seen this just recently in the Elon Musk US$44 billion offer to buy into Twitter, currently on hold, which was essentially a cash deal.

The Importance of wise cash flow management: Cash flow management is about information and skills for smarter cash decisions, planning and avoiding cash crisis and bankruptcy. I think there are basically 'survival' and 'growth' reasons for the need to manage cash flow wisely. Having sufficient and positive cash flow makes it possible for you to meet your obligations as they fall due. This is very important in making your business a credible partner to all your stakeholders.

Beyond operational 'survival', holding sufficient cash levels makes it possible for us to seize transactional opportunities as well as invest for growth at enhanced positions of negotiation and lower costs. Having sufficient cash holdings also helps in seeing us through difficult times when revenues are slow in coming. During the COVID-19 lockdown, businesses either 'benefited' from the pandemic or simply struggled to survive. Amazon and other distribution companies did well because of the opportunities the pandemic provided them whilst others in travels and hospitality like Emirates Airlines survived partly because they had cash holdings/other sources that saw them through the challenging revenue times.

Managing cash flow: Different businesses have different cash requirements. Cash requirements are in themselves dependent on several factors, such as your operating economy, industry, type of business, your business model, business cycle, trading cycle, etc. In Nigeria and many other developing economies, our use of cash for day-to-day transactions is relatively high compared to developed economies for several reasons. Some of these reasons include the fact that many individuals and even organisations do not have bank accounts. In addition, our identification systems are weak and we may not be entirely sure of the identity of the person or organisation that we may be doing business with, thereby making it near impossible to conduct non-cash transactions in which we are not protected. On the other hand, credit availability in developing economies tends to be relatively low compared to developed economies. If you are not able to access credit to help meet your temporary cash deficits, you may have no option but to keep higher cash levels in advance.

Some industries and businesses tend either to use a lot of cash or are reasonably credit-driven. If transactions in your industry are generally cash-driven, it may help you by minimising your receivables levels, but you also might not get spontaneous funding from your suppliers. Similarly, your business model impacts your cash needs. If your sales are largely on credit and/or you have a lax credit policy, you have to raise funding from other sources to meet your requirements. In addition, business and trade cycles affect your sales volume and the capacity of your customers to pay you. These, invariably, affect your cash positions and, therefore, likely cash needs.

In a basic way, the following are some of the major determinants of your cash flow position at any point in time:

- Your credit sales policy, terms, enforcement and collection of receivables,

- Inventory levels, production lead time and overall cash conversion cycle,
- Your trade terms with your suppliers which influence the levels of account payables,
- Availability and ease of non-spontaneous external funding, etc.

A key tool in helping you understand and manage your cash flow is cash flow projection.

Cash flow projection: A cash flow projection is a detailed breakdown of the inflows and outflows of cash in and out of your business over a period of time. It helps you to identify cash surplus and cash deficit points over a time scale, thereby enabling you to take appropriate actions.

To project your cash flow over a period, say, monthly for the next three years, you will need to establish your inflows, such as cash sales, credit sales collections as they fall due, etc. You then need to project all cash outflows, such as payments for purchases, payment of salaries, loan repayments, etc. Where external funding is expected to come in, that should also be captured to add to the inflows for the period. The net of your cash inflows less your cash outflows over each period is your closing cash position, which is to be carried forward to the next period as the opening balance. A negative closing balance means a cash deficit, which must be covered if you are to meet your plans and commitments, whilst a positive closing balance means a cash surplus.

Cash flow projection 'template': A simple cash flow projection table for a small business will comprise essentially several rows and columns of cash receipts and cash payments. At the top are cash receipts that add up to the total cash inflow for a period, say, a month or a year. The individual inflows might include cash sales receipts, collection of receivables, loan proceeds, etc. These are added up to give you the total cash inflows for the period. Below the rows and columns of cash inflows, you will have another set of rows and columns for cash outflows. Individual cash outflows might include purchases of materials and supplies, payment of salaries and wages, interest payments, principal loan repayments, etc. These are also added up to make the total outflow for the period. The total outflows ('B', in the Table below) are deducted from the total inflows ('A', in the Table below) to get the net cash position at the end of a period. The net cash position at the end of one period is carried forward to the beginning of the subsequent period as its opening cash position.

It should be noted that the specific composition of cash inflow sources and cash outflows may be peculiar to individual businesses. Consequently, you are to draw up your own cash projection table to meet your own plans, requirements and realities. The Table below is a sample of how a simple cash flow projection table might look like.

ABC Company
Cash Flow Projection
For the period _________ to_________

	Beginning	Period 1	Period 2	Period 3
Beginning cash/cash brought forward (₦)				

Cash receipts (₦)	Beginning	Period 1	Period 2	Period 3
Cash Sales				
Receivable collections				
Other Revenue				
Owner Investment				
Loans				
Other cash payments...				
Total cash receipts (₦) (A)				

Cash payments (₦)	Beginning	Period 1	Period 2	Period 3
Materials + Supplies				
Salaries + Wages				
Travel and Accommodation				
Interest Payment				
Principal loan repayment				
Other cash payments...				
Total cash out flow (₦) (B)				
Net cash carried forward				

Figure 12.2: Basic cash flow projection template
(© Musbahu El Yakub)

There are several simple and free cash flow projection templates that are available on the internet and can be adapted to meet your requirements. However, if you are just learning to develop a cash flow projection or are not yet proficient, I strongly suggest that you first learn to build it manually and then 'graduate' to the use of Excel before you begin to use the adaptable templates on the internet. Equally importantly, you can engage an accountant or a business consultant to help you through the exercises until you fully understand what might go into a cash projection table, how, when and which ones will not. This is very important, so that you become clear of what it takes to make the projections in varied situations. Once you get comfortable, you can begin to use the templates.

Principles and practices of wise cash flow management: I find three variables particularly important in running most businesses. These are profitability, cash flow and growth. In its simplest, profitability is about your sales revenues being greater than all the attributable costs of delivering your products or projects to your customers over a period. In the short run, a business may survive and even grow with little or no profitability as investors and creditors continue to provide required cash. But this is usually not sustainable in the long run. The immediate and long-run survival and growth of a business can only be sustained by being profitable and with positive cash flows. As it is often said, cash is truly the lifeblood of a business. Some of the principles and practices of wise cash management include:

- You should be able to make intelligent and realistic projections about the economy, your industry, business and the market.

- You must keep complete and accurate financial records. Specifically, you have to generate cash flow projections based on your plans, operational and market realities.

- You should remain alert to the objective of maintaining a positive cash flow even as you strive to maximise the profitability of your investments and operations.

- Be alert and ready for negative cash flow periods based on your projections. In such situations, you should either plan to cover up the gap in advance or cut out on certain outflows.

- Minimise credit sales and the risks associated with that. Where you need to make sales on credit, you should have a clear and firm credit control and debt collection policies and actions.

- Assess your customers and limit trade credits to only those deserving. Even as you do that, you should also ensure that you have contractual documents to protect your interests.

- Always speed up the collection of your receivables and be friends with payment officials of your customers'.

- Don't wait until due dates before you follow up with your customers on payments. Rather, begin to formally remind them of upcoming payments days and weeks in advance!

- Negotiate to enjoy trade credits from your suppliers and delay payments within the period you have, but certainly without defaulting.

- Your operations and the technology you deploy should help you facilitate receipt of payments.

- Build a good relationship with your bank and ensure that you get a standby line of credit.

- Watch out for and reduce the tendency to tie down cash in inventory and even fixed assets.

- Think through and assess each investment and payment you will be making. Negotiate and get favourable payment and repayment terms that give you generous breathing space.

- Hold on to your cash fastidiously through each payment you will be making and eliminate all waste.
- Where appropriate, consider leasing rather than the outright purchase of assets.
- Review your financial and cash position regularly.

13.0 Supply Chain Management

Every business delivers some product (goods and/or services) to its customers. To successfully achieve this, several things must be done well and correctly. These include the identification and sourcing of raw materials from external suppliers, processing of raw materials internally and delivery of the end-product to customers. The management of this 'supply chain' is critical to the survival, growth and success of any business operation and is the subject of our discussions over the next few pages.

Supply Chain Management is the handling of the flow of raw goods and services from external sources, processing them internally and delivering the finished goods and services to external customers. It involves all the aspects of getting the required input from suppliers to processing it internally and delivering output to customers.

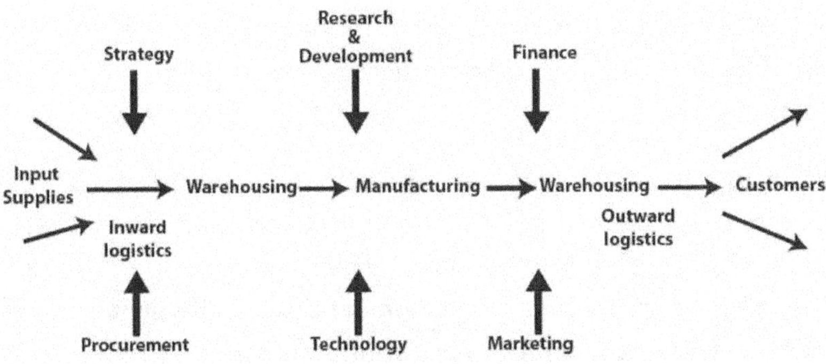

Figure 13.1: Supply chain dynamics
(© Musbahu El Yakub)

Supply chain management covers everything from product conceptualisation to development, sourcing input, production, inward and outward logistics as well as information systems for the coordination of all the activities. An optimised supply chain process makes it possible for a business to add value at every point through the following:

- Better predictions of customer demands
- Enhanced product development processes
- Increased procurement and production efficiencies
- Increased logistics effectiveness
- Improvements in quality of products
- Reduced overheads
- Cashflow improvement, etc.

The elements of Supply Chain Management are as follows:

Clear Corporate Objective: A successful supply chain management drive must start with a clear corporate objective. This is about answering the *why* of the effort. The answer to the *why* are the reasons that justify the need for an efficient and effective supply chain management process. These include the importance as well as the benefits of the process. A statement of supply chain management objective might, for instance, be *"... to ensure the timely production and delivery of required quality products to our customers at competitive prices."*

Planning: For a supply management effort to succeed and remain successful in an organisation, a supply chain plan has to be developed. The involvement of senior management as well as key operatives is crucial to the development process. Involving senior management will demonstrate commitment and give teeth to the process. On the other hand, the involvement of middle-level operators will bring out details and latent ideas as well as give them a sense of ownership of the plan.

Company-wide Development: Supply process involves all the parts of the business, from product development, market development, to production, finance and accounts, etc. Similarly, all levels of the organisation from van drivers to general managers are involved in one way or another. Consequently, it is imperative that all the sections and levels of the organisation are involved as much as is necessary and possible in the planning process mentioned above.

Regular Reviews: Change is said to be the only constant in our lives today. Accordingly, supply chain plans must be regularly reviewed for two purposes. The first purpose is to ensure that the existing plan is being carried out well. If there are unwanted and controllable variances, they should be understood and addressed. The second purpose is to ensure that new developments, either internal or external to the organisation, are captured and incorporated into the plan.

Information-driven: A supply chain management plan is only as good as the information on which it is predicated. Thus, it is necessary that reliable information form the basis of the planning process. Where assumptions are to be made, they should be intelligently developed. Changes to fundamentals should be incorporated into the regular reviews mentioned above.

Use of Technology: The incorporation and use of technology in supply chain management is now a must for most organisations. The use of technology facilitates the flow of information on real-time basis as well as processing large volumes of data. It is also used in the production, monitoring and controlling the flow of goods and services along the chain.

Beyond the elements mentioned above, most other functions of a business organisation impact and are impacted by supply management activities. As shown in the schematic above, the finance function is greatly impacted by the chain, as payments have to be made to suppliers and collected from customers, as may be agreed. The marketing function is, obviously, also impacted by supply chain activities, as raw materials have to be procured to be processed into final products in time to be delivered to customers as agreed.

There are also a few factors to be considered in developing a supply chain strategy that is required in developing the plan mentioned above. These include,

Sourcing – This is about the identification, evaluation, selection and management of supplier relationships.

Inventory Management – The management of inventory levels to meet production and marketing requirements.

Returns – Management of inward and outward returns.

Logistics – To cover the inward transportation, warehousing and outward transportation of raw materials, work-in-progress as well as finished goods, other consumables, spare parts, etc.

Cost Management – A fundamental objective of all supply chain management processes is cost management.

Customer Service – At the end, everything is about serving the customer profitably.

So far, we have introduced supply chain management responsibility, its benefits and elements as well as the factors to consider in formulating its strategy. Next, we take up the interlinkages of strategy, plan and procedures in supply chain management.

With good farm management systems, a catfish farmer might need some four months for the fingerlings to attain a weight of 2kg each. The monthly average demand may be, say, two thousand 2kg fish during the 'low periods'. But the demand surges during the Muslims' fasting month of Ramadhan as well as during Christmas and new year festivities. In addition, wedding ceremonies peak up in July and August and also in November and December, pushing up demand for catfish.

Besides the 'established' demand during the low periods, the entrepreneur will need to estimate what will be the likely demand during

Ramadhan, Christmas and New Year festivities as well as the two annual wedding peak periods. With that, the entrepreneur will need to develop a plan for the supply of the fingerlings from the hatchery in a way to have the fish attain the target 2kg weight in four months as well as uninterrupted supply of feed and medication. To achieve that as seamlessly as possible, the entrepreneur will need a supply chain strategy, a supply chain plan and supply chain procedures.

Supply Chain Strategy: We have earlier introduced planning as one of the elements of an effective supply chain management practice. However, planning cannot be carried out without first developing a strategy around which a plan is to revolve.

The supply chain strategy is the road map you have to develop to help you source the required raw materials and other supplies, establish an effective inward and outward delivery logistics system and streamline the production of your goods and services. The overriding objective of a supply chain strategy is to maximise value at each node and stage of sourcing, procurement, production and delivery. A supply chain strategy is to ensure that optimisation, efficiency, effectiveness and resilience are built into the supply chain system. Besides overall business objectives, additional factors to be considered in the development of supply chain strategy are:

- **External industrial realities, such as technology, processes and practices:** This should answer questions such as what technologies we have or should have that we can deploy or leverage on. What are the common practices and what can we do better?

- **Internal company value proposition:** This should answer questions like what our value propositions are to our customers and how we can deepen and widen them. That is, in what other ways can we extract more value?

- **Internal decision-making processes:** Internal decision-making processes are the executory components of your strategy. An excellent strategy and plan with poor execution don't achieve anything.

In the past, supply chains were built to be lean so as to minimise waste whilst only minimum investment was made in working assets, such as inventory. The on-time delivery system of Dell Computers in the 1990s made it possible for customers to 'build' their computers and place their orders online. With the orders placed, a whole set of triggers went off to ensure parts and components arrive on time to assemble the computer and meet the order. With COVID-19 experiences now, however, companies are also opting for resilience rather than just the efficiency of their supply chain systems.

To reduce your supply chain vulnerabilities, you need to factor in the following:

1. Ensure you have safety or buffer stock to absorb the impact of unexpected delays and/or surges in product demands. Safety buffer should be incorporated not just for inventory but also for time and capacity.
2. Standardising and streamlining your processes and operations will help you to achieve further efficiencies through consistency and the elimination of wastages.
3. Diversifying your sourcing, production and logistics networks will help you to absorb unforeseen disappointments from your partners.
4. If you can afford it, invest in building demand forecasting capacity that will help you to gauge the demand for materials ahead of time. Forecasting tools are available that will help you to improve your lead time, cut costs and improve customer satisfaction.

A resilient supply chain strategy will help you to deliver on your value proposition, improve productivity, manage risks and reduce costs.

Supply Chain Planning: Once you develop your supply chain strategy, the next critical responsibility is supply chain planning. It is the process of forecasting demand and planning for supplies and production to meet the demand as well as achieve corporate objectives. There are several advantages of supply chain planning, such as the reduction of operating costs, the elimination of delivery delays and production disruptions, streamlining of operations, etc. The components of supply chain planning are:

- **Sales planning:** This is about forecasting demand and planning all sales activities. The more accurate you can forecast demand for your products, the better you can plan to meet it.

- **Forecasting supply:** The objective of forecasting demand is to be able to plan for your supplies to have optimum inventory levels and at the best costs possible.

- **Production planning:** The objective of your production planning is to produce only what is required, maintain optimum inventory levels, eliminate wastages and reduce costs.

- **Operations planning:** Operations planning is about the overall coordination of cross-functional activities. This is where sales and marketing, production and all other operations units meet to ensure a perfect fit of all activities across departments and with the sole purpose of meeting customer demands and corporate objectives.

Supply Chain Procedures: Beyond having a supply chain strategy, we must have a set and series of procedures if we are to succeed in executing our plans. A supply chain 'standard operating procedure' ('SOP') is systemic instructions conceptualised, developed and formalised to guide workers in carrying out routine and non-routine duties and operations.

Supply chain SOP is developed to help to achieve overall corporate objectives. SOPs cover approval authorisations, risk management measures to minimise supply chain vulnerabilities, minimise costs and maximise value at each node and stage, achieve required quality standards and minimise handling goods as well as keep proper documentation, etc. Answers to pertinent questions must be provided on:

- **Demand forecasting:** How do we reliably forecast demand? Who/what department should do that? How often should that be done?

- **Raw materials and supplies requirements:** Given the demand forecasts that we have, what raw materials and other supplies do we need? What are the lead times for each supply? What should be our buffer stock and, therefore, reorder levels? How many alternate suppliers should we have for each material? Who/what department is to be responsible for ordering, receiving, storing and releasing raw materials/supplies?

- **Production:** Who/what department should be responsible for taking production orders? What are the lead times for production? Are there clear production records from receipt of raw materials and suppliers to manhour input, work-in-progress and finished goods records?

- **Logistics:** Who/what department shall be responsible for inward logistics from suppliers and outward logistics to customers?

- **Managing exceptions:** Who/what department shall be responsible for sending out and taking in returns? What accounting entries must be passed?

- **Procurement management:** Who/what department shall be responsible for the overall coordination of procurement activities? Are there complete records for each activity? Are contracts with suppliers duly documented, current and valid?

- **Sales management:** Are sales contracts duly negotiated with the best interests of the company at heart? Are the sales contracts documented into legally binding agreements? Are sales records, from orders, to deliveries, invoicing and payment receipts all properly and fully documented?

Supply Chain Relationship Management: Managing supplier and customer relationships are critical to business success. It is about developing, managing and growing supply chain alliances with a view to creating value systems that are mutually beneficial to all. The philosophy behind a wise supply chain relationship management is to realise and act on the basis that the success of all organisations along the supply chain is key to your own success.

Up to the late 1990s and even early 2000s, laptops were not entirely common in our country. As rooky IT entrepreneurs, we began to get orders for the supply of laptops from a major client. Whilst we had funds to meet part of what was beginning to become a regular order, we certainly didn't have all the funds we needed to procure and supply all the laptops all the time.

We came across a supplier whom we convinced to make available the laptops to us against our 30-day post-dated cheque. The kind supplier obliged. On the other side of the equation, we were able to convince the client to make payments to us within two weeks. Consequently, we never failed to pay the supplier by the time the post-dated cheque we issued was due for presentation. To reciprocate and further bond our good relationship, we directed other laptop buyers to the supplier. We went on to have a mutually rewarding relationship with the supplier for several years. Everyone was a winner.

There are about five foundations for building and managing supply chain relationships.

Integrity: For long-term and rewarding relationships with supply chain partners, the entrepreneur must always come clean. If you need raw materials on credit from your supplier, ask for that and negotiate and commit to when you settle the bill. Once you agree on a payment date, you must do everything legitimately possible and/or necessary to discharge your obligation by the agreed date. If you can establish a reputation of keeping your word, you will get all the support you may always need in business.

Be professional: You must be dispassionate in evaluating vendors that supply goods and provide services to you. Depending on your type of business, you may also need a firm assessment of your customers as well. Regardless of your business size, make sure that both your suppliers and customers take your business seriously.

Long-term perspective: Having a long-term perspective is key to building sustainably successful relationships. This involves aligning, sometimes competing, interests in a way that everyone wins.

Competence: Most businesses are significantly all about supply chain management. To succeed in building great relationships with your suppliers and customers, you must be able to deliver results. Be good at what you do and both prospective customers and suppliers will be referred to you.

A dedicated team of staff: A non-negotiable component for the success of your business is a team of dedicated staff. It is required to develop strategies and build plans as well as harmonise the activities and processes required to maximise value at the lowest cost possible.

14.0 Start Selling! Keep Selling!

"Nothing happens until a sale is made."
– Thomas Watson

All business functions are interlinked and interdependent. However, selling is the primary function that generates operational revenues, which cover costs and make profits. This very important function must be taken seriously by every entrepreneur.

What is selling? Ordinarily, selling refers to any transaction in which money is exchanged for a product between a seller and a buyer. In our context, the seller is the business organisation that makes a product available to a buyer, who pays for it. Technically, however, selling comprises all the personal and impersonal activities involved in identifying, creating, developing and growing the demand for a given product.

The importance of selling: Selling is about facilitating exchange between a buyer and a seller. The buyer gets a desired value while the seller receives payment, which covers their cost and makes them a profit. But between this seemingly cold exchange, the staff of a business have been paid salaries, suppliers of raw materials would have been paid, etc. Similarly, at the end of everything, value-added and corporate taxes are paid to government. The cash from profitable sales is a critical asset and resource that keeps a company afloat (other cash sources such as equity from shareholders and debt from creditors can easily dry up if there are no prospects for sustainable sales revenues.) Invariably, it is sales that create jobs and wealth and make investments attractive.

How do you sell? Whatever your business, it is fundamental that you take selling seriously. There are a few factors that will determine the success of your sales effort, as follows:

- **Understand the selling process:** The selling process starts from your 'prospecting', 'preparation/pre-approach', 'approach', 'presentation', 'handling objectives', 'closing' and 'follow-up'. Understanding the requirements and challenges of each stage will help you to prepare well in advance, thereby enhancing your ability to meet the customers' needs and improving your chances of success.

- **Understand your customers and what they want:** Your ability to serve your customers well depends on the extent to which you understand them. Listen to and observe your customers. Often, you have to be on the same page with your customers and offer them what they desire. Other times you have to be ahead of them and give them solutions and conveniences that they hadn't even thought of!

- **Offer saleable products:** A major challenge in every business is to ensure that the product (physical good or service) that you offer is saleable. Prior to product development and launches, you will need to conduct a diligent feasibility study and build a sound business plan. There are many ways of selling products successfully. Sometimes it is simply about 'tweaking' product features, presentation or the service attached to that. Other times, companies succeed by inventing completely new products. It is your calling to decide how you believe you will succeed. No matter the option you are taking though, the ultimate objective and challenge are to achieve a sufficient volume of sales of the product to cover your running costs and deliver profits, except for loss-leading products, which serve a different purpose altogether.

- **Assemble the right sales team:** As with most professions, there are technical and emotional requirements to successful selling. Getting the right sales team or building and developing one is an absolute must in your organisation. If you have the right sales team the members of which are always excited and happy selling, you are a head start away from your competitors.

Sometimes, we sell 'commodities' that are also offered by others. But even in such situations, we should be clear about what the 'unique selling proposition' ('USP') of our product is. The USPs of a product are the compelling benefits that make it stand out from the competition. It gives the customer a good and irresistible reason to select your product rather than that from the competition. It is important you are clear about what your USPs are.

- **Prime your enterprise to sell:** Another key to success is to ensure that your whole company is primed to sell. The idea is that you should educate and get all staff to have the 'selling mentality'. From your front desk right down to the back-end of your operations, all staff must support marketing and sales efforts. However, this is not to say that all staff will be directly involved in sales negotiations and logistics! Rather, it just means that all staff must support the sales effort within their specific role or function. For instance, the inventory control officer must process their papers timely and correctly to ensure a quick release of the product, whilst the despatch officer must ensure safe and timely delivery to the right customer.

- **Market your product:** Regardless of how good your products and people are, you are to be aware of how to play around with the so-called 4Ps of marketing to facilitate the selling function. These are:
    - o Product: A comprehensive understanding of what product you are offering as well as its features, benefits and competitive positioning.

- o Place: A detailed understanding of the best place(s) to make the product available to your customers.
- o Price: This is the price-value proposition of your product; how it compares with competition as well as an articulated customer attraction strategy.
- o Promotion: This articulates the best approaches to reaching and delivering all marketing messages to customers.

- **Think long-term:** Your long-term selling success will be conditional upon your ability to think and act long-term. In thinking and acting long-term, you aim to balance conflicting needs and avoid pitching your interests against that of your customers. By thinking long-term, you will very likely forego taking undue advantage of your customers which will come back to haunt you. The way to make this possible is through:
  - o Integrity: Ensure that you deal with your customers fairly on all issues. Do not allow possible short-term gains to becloud your vision on the need for a long-term relationship that all parties will be happy with.
  - o Build loyalty: You should ensure that you are considerate of the long-term needs of customers and will not sacrifice that for your own short-term 'gains'.
  - o Impress your customers: Work to over-deliver above your agreed commitments to your customers. If you can frequently 'wow' your customers, you stand a good chance to hold them for long.

- **Make continuous improvements:** Remember that nothing is static in life. Your wonderful product, your highly effective marketing strategy, your team of loyal, dedicated and competent staff, etc. can all be bested within a short period by the competition. Consequently, you should adopt a strategy of continuous learning and improvement in all the components of your selling effort. From product conceptualisation to sales, ensure that you up the ante on your own before your competition catches up and/or beats you. You should be comfortable and adept at raising the bar on your own rather than resting on your laurels and allowing the competition to do that. Remember, it is a lot easier to retain your customers than to get new ones. So, it pays to keep them!

15.0 Customer Service

The sales and marketing functions in a business organisation are key in generating operating revenues for a business. But a significant component of the value proposition of most businesses, that is desired by customers, is customer service.

When we make choice between one airline and another or between one restaurant and another, the service we get tends to be a major factor in our choice. But while this factor is not restricted to airlines and restaurants, my experience and observation with most budding entrepreneurs and those seeking to grow their businesses is that they tend to focus disproportionately more on raising cash, supply chain management, production, etc. Yes, indeed all those functions are crucial to success. However, the quality of customer service a business is able to provide is a critical determinant of the level of revenues that can be generated over an extended period. How can you, therefore, develop a bias and culture for great customer service in your company?

Understand what customer service is: Customer service is the totality of the experience that results from all interactions between a customer and your company as you make a product available to them. This experience starts from what the customer sees on your website to the phone call they put through to your business to make enquiries to learn about what you can offer, the actual delivery of the product to the customer and the post-purchase service, as may be required.

Benefits of great customer services: It is taken as given that whatever products you offer to your customers must meet certain quality expectations of theirs at the minimum. Beyond that, what attracts and keeps customers' patronage is largely their experiences in dealing with you. Wonderful customer experiences are directly linked to the repeat business they can conduct with you and the referrals they can make of your products to friends, family and colleagues. In addition, great customer service can justify premium pricing and put you ahead of your competitors. The beneficial consequences of all of that are better customer relations, increased turnover, profitability and growth.

How do you go about building a culture of great customer service in your business?

Understand your customers: To be able to serve your customers very well, you have to first understand them well! What are the customers actually looking for when they buy your product? What utility do they hope to derive? Are you able to identify the technical and emotional components of the buying process and decisions of the customers? What are their expectations in terms of pricing, product quality, delivery, etc.? Study the customers and ask them questions!

Understand the lifetime value of the customer: We have elsewhere introduced the concept of customer lifetime value ('CLV') as the present value of the projected cash flows that can be made out of a customer over the entire relationship. CLV looks beyond individual transactions with a customer into the totality of what could be made out of the customer into the future.

Understanding the lifetime value of customers is important because it justifies and encourages businesses to shift their focus from achieving only short-term benefits, which may be to the detriment of future benefits, to the long-term loyalty of customers. Their long-term loyalty will enhance sales and profitability for your business. Similarly, CLV sets an upper limit on the investments that can be made to acquire new customers as well as retain existing ones. A clear understanding of customers' lifetime values will make it worth your while to do what needs to be done to serve your customers well at known costs knowing the benefits that you will gain over time.

Train all employees on the art and science of great customer service: It is common for employees to dichotomise themselves into 'customer contact' and 'backend' staff. Whilst some employees might practically be back-end staff that hardly get in contact with customers, what they do invariably impacts on overall customer experience. From the conduct of your customer contact employees to those at the backend, everyone does something that contributes to or hurts customer experiences.

Train all your staff regardless of their actual direct responsibility to appreciate the significance of customers to the success of your business. Train each of your staff to positively view each customer contact, directly or indirectly, as an opportunity to live your brand promise. The level of the preparation of your employees to handle both routine and special requirements of your customers is critical to the effectiveness of these interactions. Ironically, even when things go wrong we can get great opportunities to redeem ourselves from our customers by doing what is right beyond their expectations. By making all employees customer-centric in their thinking and actions, we improve or sales revenues and profitability through strong customer loyalty.

One of the big issues in our environment is the unwillingness of entrepreneurs and their managers to suffer transactional losses to the detriment of their relationships with customers. The common remark in such situations is 'Ah, I can't lose money'. But sometimes, the right and wise thing to do is to suffer those transient losses if that will strengthen our relationships with our customers. What is important is to ensure that if an error was made, the cause of the error is understood and avoided in the future. Sometimes, absorbing one-off losses to maintain relationships is in our long-term business interests. That is why large corporations, such as Toyota, Samsung, etc. could easily recall thousands of cars and mobile phones due to some factory faults at great costs to the corporations. At their end, however, the corporations know that they are building a reputation of trust and reliability with their customers that will more than compensate for their short-term losses.

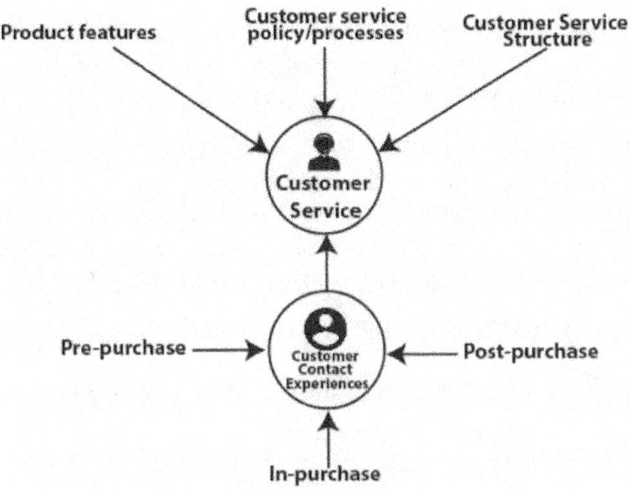

15.1: Customer service factors
(© Musbahu El Yakub)

Design a structure geared to serve the customer: Beyond training your staff on customer service, your company's organizational structure and procedures should ease and facilitate your customer service strategy. Your controls and procedures should be designed to protect the company but also serve the customers without their suffering delays or undue inconveniences. Thankfully, some of the best things in life and in business are easy. You should, therefore, design a simple but effective structure for fair and quality service to customers.

The features of a customer service-oriented organisation include:

- The most senior executives sincerely believe in the doctrine of customer service and they live it, thereby showing examples to the middle level and junior employees.

- Employees are always happy serving customers. They work as seamless teams determined to make the customers' experience wonderful. Turf wars and claims and counterclaims for credits are minimal.

- They always want to improve the quality, features and benefits of their products and the effectiveness of their service delivery. They do not wait for the customer to first get frustrated before they change and improve. They force positive change on themselves internally.

- They are consistent in delivering excellent service. The customer always leaves feeling great about the experience. Inconsistency kills customer loyalty!

- They always strive to surpass their customers' expectations,

- They are accurate in handling transactions. Furthermore, they try to do the right and correct thing first time and always.

- They make good use of technology to serve their customers.

- When things go wrong, as they sometimes do, customer-centric organisations respond quickly, communicating sincerely, timely and fully to those affected or likely to be affected and telling them what is being done to remedy the situation.

Great customer service is real. There are many companies in real life, from different industries and of those different sizes that thrive on deliberate customer-centrism. They can be corner shops, bakeries, airlines, banks, hotel chains, construction companies, recruitment agencies, computer companies, etc. Work to build your company into a great customer service machine.

16.0 Branding

"Your brand is what other people say about you when you are not in the room." – Jeff Bezos

We have mentioned severally that business is about making available products (goods and services) which solve problems, create conveniences and/or opportunities for customers. To achieve commercial success in the marketplace, you need to create value through the goods and services you provide. Within and beyond creating value, however, you need to build an identity that will stand you out from the crowd. This identity and how you go about building and protecting it is termed branding.

As little boys and girls in the past, every toothpaste was 'Macleans' to us; Every tea was 'Lipton'. This was the extent of successful branding by GlaxoSmithKline (later by Beecham and SKB) and Unilever (later Argyll Foods and Pepsi Lipton International), respectively. Today, the most valuable brands in the world include Apple, Amazon, Microsoft, Samsung, Coca-Cola, Toyota, etc. These companies are able not only to reach their audiences but also connect with them. Beyond 'reach' and 'connection', these brands are considered trustworthy and reliable by their customers. Successful brands are generally responsible corporate citizens, delivering services to their communities and the public beyond their commercial and fiduciary obligations. Closer home, we see how successful brands in Nigeria, from Dangote Group to BUA, UBA, Zenith, etc. are also reasonably socially responsive. During the COVID-19 pandemic, these companies provided great support to the government and the Nigerian public.

What is Branding? In a limited sense, branding is generally seen in terms of company and product name(s), symbol, catchphrase, etc. But beyond that, branding is the process through which a business makes itself known to its customers as well as how it differentiates itself from the competition. The objective of all branding activities is to create a pleasant, attractive and quality identity that customers are happy and excited to associate with. Brand development takes place at various levels like company level, product group level, individual product level, etc.

The brand you are able to create will consist of all the features that distinguish and put your products ahead of the products that your competitors offer to the same market. These features will generally be a combination of tangible and intangible components. Visual features will include elements, such as logo, colours, packaging, etc. Distinctive features will include quality, personality and the character of your products while intangible aspects will include customers' experiences with your goods and services.

Figure 16.1: Coca-Cola – Known and recognised all over the world
(Photo credit – Jonathan Borba from Pexels)

The Benefits of Effective Branding: The benefits of effective branding are multi-fold. They include the following:

Customer Recognition: Billions of people on this planet can identify the Coca-Cola bottle. When customers can identify a brand's colours, logos, etc., they are more likely to choose them over other competing products no matter how much better the latter might be. The ease with which customers identify a product is an indication of the strength of the brand.

Customer Loyalty: Excellent branding has a way of attracting customers to your products. Think about how many times you have accepted certain products on the strength of their presentation, packaging, quality reputation and the referral of other customers. Beyond attracting new customers, excellent branding helps to achieve overall high customer retention rates.

Brand Equity: Customer loyalty, as mentioned above, makes the introduction of new products by reputable brands much easier than if companies didn't have loyal customers. Sony introducing the Walkman or Apple introducing the iPod are good examples of companies doing very well with their new products because of their existing reputations. If customers are loyal to your brand, they will be attracted to your new products as well as serve as your ambassadors to non-users.

Attracts Talent: Building a reputable brand helps companies to attract excellent staff and influencers. Having the right talent within and around your system is necessary if you are to keep developing and introducing new products that attract and retain customers.

Keeps You ahead of Your Competitors: The ultimate benefit of excellent branding is in helping you to stay ahead of the competition through customer patronage. The more accepted your brand is by customers and the general public, the more patronage in new and repeat sales you will attract.

A Brand is an Asset: In the long run, nothing beats an excellent reputation. We see this in the way customers 'trust' the goods and services they buy from some companies but not from others. Excellent reputation, as a result of being true to brand value, is an asset that attracts the appropriate pricing of goods and services as well as the premium valuation of a company.

Elements of Branding: To be able to navigate the initiating and ongoing processes of building and sustaining a brand, it is important to understand the features of branding:

It is about your identity: Creating a brand starts from the basics of coming up with an appropriate name, symbol, design, catchphrase, etc. It is about creating a physical and emotional identity of your company and products in the minds of your customers and the public.

It is a mindshare: Branding is about creating a position for your company and products in the minds of customers and the public through shared values. The more unique the position the stronger your brand identity.

It is a promise: Branding is not just about the perceptions you want the customers to have about your company and products, it is also a promise and commitment you make to the customers and public about who and what you are.

'Brands are Created'

"Products are made in a factory, but brands are created in the mind."
– Walter Landor

The process of shaping an envisioned, desirable perception about your business and products is what brand development is all about.

Regardless of the size or complexity of your business, the principles of brand development are the same even if the stakes might, obviously, vary. You have to be thoughtful and deliberate in developing a strategy that creates an identity, delivers on your promise and holds a mindshare of the customer and other stakeholders. At the end of everything, all brand development activities are about positioning and communication and should include the following:

Understand your business: Understanding your business is the first step to developing your brand strategy. *What business are you really into? Are you selling to middlemen and distributors or are you selling to end-users?* Understanding your business also means understanding your competitors, industry and market. Understanding your competitors and what they are doing is critical to doing things better than them.

What can you deliver? Beyond understanding your competitors and industry, you must also understand your customers. Understanding your customers is fundamental to knowing what you can do to attract and retain their loyalty. This includes knowing what they *really* want and how and where they want it. Price points and quality expectations are particularly important to varying degrees with different customers.

Understand the pathways to earning customers' loyalty: Generally, there are just two interwoven pathways to customers' minds. There is a technical pathway and an emotional pathway. The technical pathway is about such variables as the physical quality of your products, price, service response, etc. On the other hand, the emotional pathway is about the soft relationship management issues between your business and your customers.

Plan for long-term relationships: The way to building brands in a way that all stakeholders, from customers to suppliers, financiers, etc. want to do business always with you is by thinking long-term on issues. Thinking long-term helps you do what is right no matter the transient inconveniences. This is key to earning the loyalty of your customers.

Be authentic: Don't just 'copy and paste' what others are doing without being innovative by differentiating your business. Not only would 'copy and paste' commoditise you, but you may also appear artificial and unexciting. True, we may deliver the same products as others, but we can always differentiate ourselves through our services. We see this often in restaurants. The food and drinks might all be similar. But the ambience and the service offered by one restaurant simply distinguishes itself from others and with that comes higher prices for which their discerning clients gladly pay.

Don't forget the designs! Obviously, building a brand also means developing a business or product's name, logo, tagline, website content, etc. Take your time and consult with professionals who will advise you. Usually, the simpler the better. Taking into consideration market nuances and sentiments is important in design concepts.

Communicate! There are two aspects of communications that should be achieved in brand development: reach and connection. Reach is about getting to both your current and potential customers while connection is about ensuring that you achieve the desired objective of the reach.

One of the common communication errors that I see in our environment is that of the literal translation of English expressions into local languages or the literal translations of expressions in one local language into another! This not only misses the 'connection' object of communication but shows a lack of diligence and professionalism. If you feel it is relevant to deliver English catchphrases in a local language, the appropriate thing to do is to get the equivalent, not the literal translation, of the phrase in that language. It should be the same thing if you wish to achieve the duplicate objective across two local languages.

Beyond the strategy and actual development of your brand, a few other actions are necessary:

'Care and Feeding': It is not sufficient that a good brand is developed. It must be nurtured and protected through 'care and feeding'. Care and feeding are about delivering and standing by the promised value at all times. A specific aspect of 'care and feeding' is to ensure that you do not water down the quality and standards of your brand through reckless price discounts as a result of competitive pressures. Just think of the consequences of Apple struggling to compete with the lower-end smartphones and computers.

Realignment: Building a brand takes time. However, it happens that for perfectly legitimate reasons, certain changes must be incorporated from time to time. You can, therefore, consider brand realignments in tandem with emerging realities. Otherwise, the longevity of brand focus is a measure of the strength of a brand DNA.

Toyota Motor Corporation is one of the most successful car manufacturing companies in the world. Over the 'short years' of its life, it has surpassed many older car manufacturing companies through innovation and customer-centric focus. Toyota's patented manufacturing methods, known as Toyota Production System ('TPS'), which form the core of its manufacturing strategy, are built on three key philosophies viz; Customer first, Employee satisfaction and Company stability. The objectives of TPS are to achieve the highest quality at the lowest cost in the shortest lead time possible. At the end of everything, TPS is about delivering quality products at affordable prices to various sub-classes of customers for decades on end.

17.0 Value-Add, Costing and Pricing

Sometime ago, I was involved with a Company that was bidding for a project. I worked with them and we submitted both the Technical and Financial bid components. After scaling the Technical stage, the Company was invited by the Client for negotiations of the contract terms because the Company had the lowest financial offer amongst all the companies that bade for the project.

In the course of the negotiations, the Client asked why the Company had a 'low quote' (the next lowest financial bid was over eight times the Company's!) I responded on behalf of the Company that, "Even at that seemingly 'low quote', the project is satisfactorily profitable to the Company". Simple. The Company got the job and successfully executed it. Everyone was happy. And I have no doubt that if the Client has a similar project in the future, the Company will be preferred.

The above 'concern' by the Client brings out a reality in the costing and pricing philosophies of many individuals and organisations in our environment: Every business opportunity is about maximizing profit. But even beyond that, we tend to think that every business transaction is about us making all the money we can to solve all our financial problems at one go! It is like each transaction, irrespective of its details, must take us out of our poverty and make us 'stinking' rich!

This costing mindset and pricing model are, sadly, rampant in all strata of our society. From the mechanic that will fix the office car to the carpenter who is asked to quote to produce furniture for a soon-to-be-wedded couple or the contractor that is invited to submit a financial bid for the building of a school block for a state government. We just want to get rich overnight.

Whilst it is legitimate to maximise the profit you can make on transactions, it must be done wisely, taking into consideration three things: First, your pricing should take into account both the value you are actually delivering and the price at which your competition can also deliver the same service. Second, you shouldn't be too greedy as to risk losing the business entirely because you stupidly believe one transaction should solve all your financial problems! Third, your pricing should be fair in a way that it is acceptable to your client whilst, of course, being profitable to you.

If any of those conditions are not met, you risk losing the business or if you get the business, your relationship with the client can be jeopardised if they (and they can) eventually find out that they could have gotten better pricing for the same service from elsewhere. Remember that un-happy or customers that feel cheated wouldn't come back to you and neither would they make referrals to you.

How do you avoid the risks mentioned above?

Long-term relationships are beneficial: We expound in this book that the sustainably-successful entrepreneur is one that views and manages their relationships with their employees, clients, regulators, etc. on a long-term basis. Having a long-term perspective on business relationships makes us circumspect, cautious and fair in our dealings without losing focus on our business objectives.

Understand the difference between value, cost and price: The entrepreneur needs to have a sound understanding of the difference and linkages between the value they offer, their operational cost structure and costing process as well as their pricing model. These four variables are key to relationship development, sustainable profitability and wealth creation…

The essence of every business is to provide products (goods and/or services) to a group of customers (individuals and/or organisations) called a 'market' and in the process generate wealth. To stand a good chance of generating wealth, a business needs to be able to create a desired value. The value created by a business is represented by the features in the products that the company offers to its customers. 'Economic value' is a measure of the benefit that is derivable from a product by a customer. Economic value, however, does not mean that the utility derived by the customer is necessarily financial. No. For instance, a wealthy person could buy a Rolex wristwatch for millions of Naira not because of any financial benefit they can derive from the watch but for, perhaps, the feeling they get from owning the prized item. The point is that the 'economic value' we ascribe to a product could be derived from some social, psychological or of course monetary benefit that we enjoy from it. Measured in units of currency, it is the amount a customer is willing to pay for a product and may be higher or lower than its market value as represented by its market price.

The profitable pricing of products is critical to wealth creation. Most business operations price their products on a cost plus a margin basis. This means the total cost attributable to the value on offer is established and then a pre-determined margin is added to come up with a price. It should be noted, however, that there may be realistic constraints to this approach. If, for instance, a product you want to offer is already available in the market at some price, you may not just be able to offer yours at a higher price without a corresponding, justifiable and perceptible value differential. Regardless, there are several ways of determining the cost of the value you provide. But your type of business will influence how you establish your costs. The cost components and the costing process of a furniture business will be different from those of a restaurant and also from that of a medical facility. The principles are, however, basically all the same.

So far, we have brought out the need for the entrepreneur to have a captive costing method and a wise pricing model in their business. To be able to achieve these dual objectives, we need to understand the difference and relationships between the trio of value, cost and price.

Value, Cost and Price

'Price is what you pay. Value is what you get.'
– Warren Buffett

Value: The value your business creates is about the features of the product (goods and/or services) it produces or provides. From a customer's point of view, however, value is a measure of the benefit that is derivable from a product. As a business, therefore, you have not created any value if the customer doesn't not see any benefit in your product for which they will be willing to pay a price. Furthermore, value is personal and about the worth the customer attributes to a product, which can differ from one person to another. At an auction, we see an artwork ultimately purchased for a couple of millions of dollars by a particular collector when some of those who participated in the auction had already dropped out at a just few hundreds of thousands of dollars.

The entrepreneur must be clear about the features of their product that give it a selling proposition. *Which features of your product are actually valued by customers? Which features add to product costs but aren't valued by the customers?* A core objective is to always ensure that the sum of the costs of the input value a business brings from outside and the input value it creates/adds inside are less than the value of the final product it delivers to the market, as shown below.

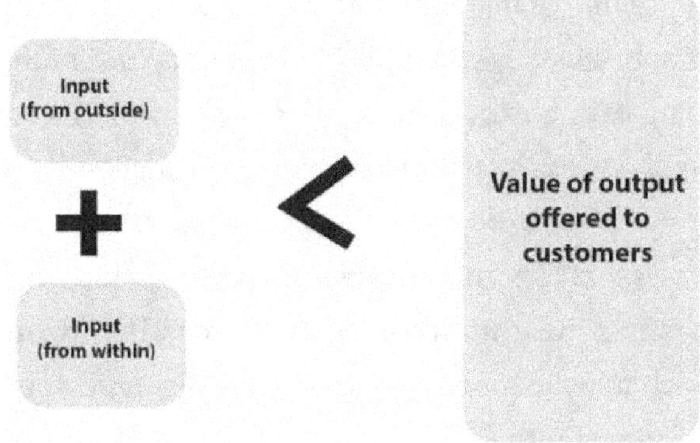

Figure 17.1: Positive value principle
(© Musbahu El Yakub)

Cost: Costs can be broken down into 'direct' and 'indirect'. Direct cost ('DC') are all the costs associated with the direct manufacture of a product on the factory floor. They comprise direct materials ('DM') and direct labour ('DL') costs. Direct materials refer to all the materials that go into the manufacture of your product by applying direct labour and factory overheads ('FOH'). For a shoe production business, that will include the hide, the thread, the wood and other accessories that go directly into the shoe. Direct labour refers to all the labour on the factory floor that is involved in directly manufacturing the finished goods from raw materials. Direct labour costs include the salaries, wages and benefits that are paid to this labour force. Factory overheads refer to the indirect expenses related to manufacturing the finished product, but which are not easily or directly traceable to a unit of production. Factory overheads comprise indirect materials ('IDM'), such as grease for machinery; indirect labour ('IDL'), such as factory quality assurance staff, production supervisors, etc.; and other factory overheads ('OFOH') that fall neither under indirect materials and nor under indirect labour. They may include, for instance, factory equipment depreciation. Finally, we have another class of indirect costs called selling, general and admin ('SGA') expenses. Understanding your business cost composition and structure is fundamental to developing your business strategy. *How does your cost compare to that of your competition? Which costs can you cut out or reduce to the barest minimum? How do certain cost elements trigger increments in your sales revenue?* There are different costing methods, such as **process costing, product costing, batch costing, project costing,** etc. Each may be more appropriate for one type of businesses or situation than another.

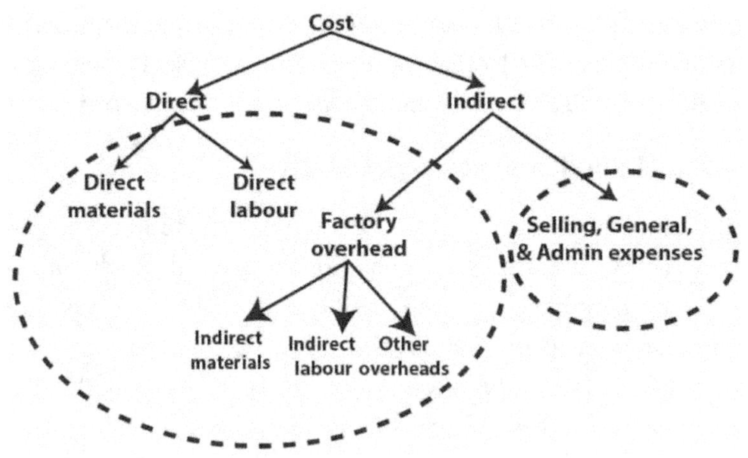

Figure 17.2: Cost components
(© Musbahu El Yakub)

Price: The price of your product is the currency value which your customers pay to acquire the product you offer. It is your financial 'reward' for providing the product. But it should be noted that the market price you are paid may be higher or lower than the value a customer actually attributes to the product. For instance, a customer may gladly pay you five thousand Naira, being the market price, for the pair of shoes you produced but are, perhaps, actually willing to pay seven thousand Naira if that was the price. In such a situation, the value of the shoe to them is higher than its market price. On the other hand, they may also purchase the same shoe at five thousand Naira only begrudgingly because there is no alternative. But left to them, the pair shouldn't be worth more than three thousand Naira. In this situation, the customer values your product less than the market price.

There are different ways businesses price their products based on pricing objectives and pricing strategies. The objectives might be **profit-related, sales-related, competition-related, customer-related**, etc. The strategies, on the other hand, include **cost-plus pricing, market-oriented pricing** and **dynamic pricing**.

Profitability and wealth creation depend on the value you create, the value as perceived by the customer, the cost at which you create the value and the price at which you are able to sell the product.

Costing Methods and Pricing Strategies

Profitability and wealth creation through value addition are two core objectives of businesses. The value you provide is what makes your customers happy, thereby making them want to buy more from you as well as make referrals to you. For the customer to be happy, the *price* they willingly pay must be worth less than the value they perceive to receive. For the business to be successful, the *cost* of providing value to customers must be less than the price the business asks, except in some exceptional situations.

Profitability and wealth creation are described by two simple equations. The first equation is that 'Total Sales ('TS') minus Total Costs ('TC') equals Profit ('TP')'. Mathematically, we can write that as TS – TC = TP. The second equation is that 'Total Assets ('TA') equals owners' Equity ('EQ') plus total Other Liabilities ('LB')'. Mathematically, that can be written as, TA = EQ + LB.

Wealth creation over time, as revealed by the second equation, is a function of profitability, which increases owners' equity and, therefore, the total assets of the business, assuming that liabilities do not grow at a faster rate. The profitability of an operation, as revealed in the first equation, is a function of the price of a unit of each product we sell, the volume of each product we have sold and the total cost of providing the product(s).

Clearly, it is necessary that an entrepreneur be able to keep a tab on the profitability of their business operation by always establishing and monitoring what their costs are vis-à-vis their sales. But industries and businesses differ in their nature as well as in the processes involved in producing their goods and services. In fact, even in the same business, situations may warrant that different transactions are costed differently.

Costing methods: We have, so far, brought out and defined two major cost categories viz, direct and indirect costs. In addition, costs can also be classified as *variable* or *fixed*. There are also certain costs that fall somewhere between those two ends of the spectrum and are called *semi-variable, semi-fixed* or *mixed* costs. Basically, variable costs are those cost components that change in tandem with how much a company produces and sells. This means that variable costs increase or decrease as output increases or decreases, respectively. On the other hand, fixed costs are those costs that remain reasonably the same regardless of output. These costs may include rent, insurance, depreciation, some type of labour costs, etc. Direct costs are typically variable while the indirect tend to be fixed. A semi-variable cost has both fixed and variable components.

Costing methods refer to a system of ascertaining and accounting for costs in any type of operation. There are several costing methods, such as Batch Costing, Unit Costing, Service Costing, Composite Costing, etc. For our purposes, we will consider two basic, yet widely applicable, methods known as '**job costing**' and '**process costing**'.

Job Costing is defined by ICMA as "*that form of specific order costing which applies where work is undertaken to customers' 'special requirements'*". (Specific Order Costing is defined by the same Institute as "*the category of basic costing methods applicable where work consists of separate contracts, jobs, or batches each of which is authorised by a special order or contract.*") In job costing, the costs of each job, from initiation to completion and delivery, are ascertained and accumulated separately, thereby making it possible to establish the profit or loss on each job.

The objective of the job costing method is to ensure that all costs are allocated appropriately and captured under the various categories discussed earlier viz, material costs, labour costs and overheads.

Businesses that apply job costing method tend to be those that carry out production based on customer specifications. They include heavy industries like shipbuilding, heavy machine foundry, etc. and also basic services like automobile repair garage, printing press, etc.

The documents needed for job costing include the *job order*, which authorises the production department to produce the item(s) that constitute the job; a *Job card, cost sheet* or *worksheet* in which all the costs incurred in the various stages of the production are captured. In addition, there are likely to be other relevant supporting documents, such as *material requisition slips, time tickets,* etc., which provide input and details for the worksheet.

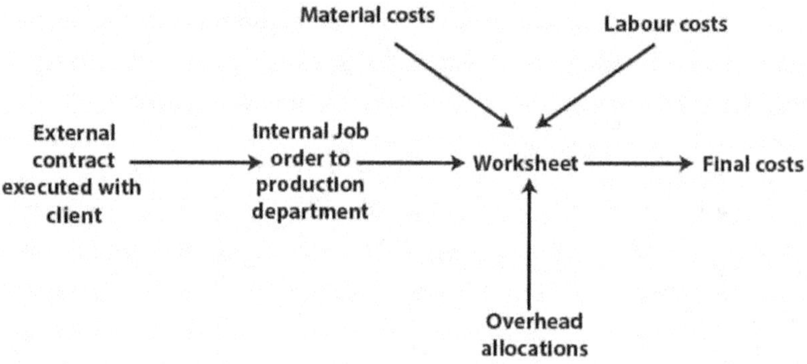

Figure 17.3: Simplified cost flow
(© Musbahu El Yakub)

The materials costs will cover all the materials used. Subject to internal policy, abnormal material loss, if any, is also charged directly. But scrap costs are generally charged to overhead cost pool, which is allocated later. For labour costs, direct labour is traced and charged to specific jobs whilst indirect labour is charged to overhead cost pool and then allocated to various open jobs depending on the measure of cost usage. Overhead costs are accumulated into one or more overhead cost pools from whence they are allocated to open jobs and like indirect labour based on the measure of cost usage. Historical costs and time on the job are usually good guide and basis for overhead cost allocations.

Process Costing: Some industries and businesses produce a large quantity of identical goods by processing raw materials (and work-in-progress, 'WIP') through a number of interlinked but distinct stages. Typically, raw materials and WIP pass through the production line in a continuous flow from an initial stage at the starting point to a final stage at the end. Process costing is suitable in such businesses as sugar refineries, petrochemicals, candy production, etc.

ICMA defines Process Costing as a *"... form of operation costing which applies where standardised goods are produced."* (The same Institute defines operation costing as *"... the category of basic costing methods applicable where standardised goods or services result from a sequence of repetitive and more or less continuous operations or process which costs are charged before being averaged over the units produced during the period."*)

Even as production is standardised and continuous, each process stage is distinct, as it takes the output from a previous stage as its input. After processing at that stage, the output serves as the input to the next production stage. Costs are compiled by preparing an account for each process. To determine the unit cost of output at the end of each stage, the total production cost of the stage is divided by the total quantity of the output at that stage over, usually, a time period. Below is a simple process costing schematic.

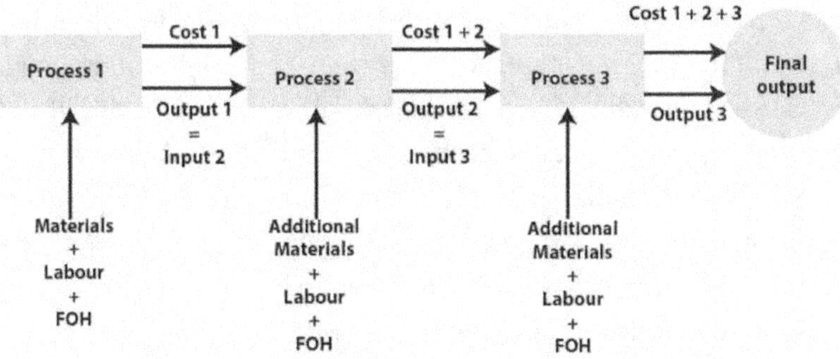

Figure 17.4: Process cost flow
(© Musbahu El Yakub)

Where there are losses, such as due to, for instance, spoilage or evaporation, the loss is first classified as either 'normal' or 'abnormal'. The cost of normal losses is absorbed by the good units completed, which will obviously increase the final average cost per unit. If the loss is, however, deemed abnormal, it will be valued as a 'good unit' and then debited to an 'Abnormal Loss Account'.

The objective of every costing method or system is to come up with a figure that is a true and 'fair' capture of what you have invested in terms of material, labour and factory overheads. But that will only give your production cost or your 'cost of goods sold', 'CoGS'. Beyond your CoGS, you must also capture what we mentioned earlier as Selling, General and Admin ('SGA') expenses. In the midst of everything, your ultimate objective is that your sales revenue must cover your CoGS to make you a gross profit. And beyond making a gross profit, you also need to cover your SGA to make a net profit before taxes.

Often, it happens in our environment that we pass the cost of our personal and business inefficiencies and failures on to the customer. That is wrong in the short-term and unsustainable in the long run. Consequently, a business must strive to be excellent at effectively providing its products to its customers efficiently. To partly do that, costing must be done carefully and taken seriously and fairly. If you don't capture all your costs, you stand a high risk of losing money by selling your products at a price that doesn't make you any profit. If, on the other hand, your business is inefficient and costing method is not 'fair', you will end up rendering your business uncompetitive. This happens when, as a result of your unnaturally high cost, you end up pricing your products much higher than your competition without any value differential perceivable and acceptable to your customers. This is a major cause of losing the trust and ultimate patronage of your customers.

Pricing: There are different ways businesses price their products based on *pricing objectives* and *pricing strategies*. The objectives might be profit-related, sales-related, competition-related, customer-related, etc. The strategies, on the other hand, include cost-plus pricing, market-oriented pricing and dynamic pricing.

Profit-related pricing objectives refer to the focus of a business management to make profit. Whilst this might seem to go without saying, the reality is that there are times when a product could be deliberately sold at a price that wouldn't make it profitable to the business. This happens, for instance, in loss leader pricing scenarios. Loss leader pricing is a pricing strategy that involves selling a product at a price that is not profitable for the purposes of attracting new customers or selling other products to prospective and/or existing customers.

If your goal is profit-driven, your company can set product pricing based on a particular profit target either on absolute basis or in terms of return on investment made or just a percentage mark-up. Generally speaking, a profit-related objective leads to a cost-plus pricing strategy. This means that after the cost of the product is determined, the entrepreneur will then add a mark-up to set a price on any basis, as mentioned above.

A costing process that is simple, yet robust and a pricing strategy that is wise are key to profitable operations and wealth creation.

Competition-related Pricing: This is a pricing objective in which the price of a product is set in some tandem with the price of competing product(s). Competition-based pricing focusses entirely on the publicly available information about the price of similar product offered by competitor(s). This pricing objective might seem simple and low risk, but because it doesn't compare actual value delivered by each competitor, you either run the risk of *missing* out on opportunities or entirely *killing* opportunities for yourself. You risk missing opportunities where your products deliver more value but you price yourself at the same level with your competitors'. You kill your opportunities entirely by overpricing yourself when your products actually offer less value than the competitors' products you benchmark against. Competition-related pricing will only be profitable and successful if you offer the same value as your competitors and your cost is lower than the price.

Market-oriented pricing strategy is the pragmatic way of pricing your product if you have a competition-related pricing objective. But rather than blindly offering your product at the same price as your competitors' regardless of value differences, you instead segment your competitors according to their value offers and prices. You then assess your value proposition and based on that decide whether to offer your product at, below or above the price of your competition.

Where you position your product pricing should be consequent upon some clear market objective. For instance, if you want to penetrate the market, you could decide to introduce your product at a price lower than equivalent/competing products. In doing this, however, you must be alert and ready to the prospects of a price war. On the other hand, if you don't want to trigger a price war, you could price like your competitors. Yet, another possibility is to differentiate your product by offering it at a higher price than the competition's if you are able to offer some additional perceptible value.

Dynamic pricing, 'demand' or 'time-based pricing' is a pricing strategy that involves setting product prices based on real-time demand. Here, the business is flexible in its pricing, depending on consumer purchasing habits or current market demands. Factors to take into consideration in this pricing strategy include supply and demand dynamics as well as competitor pricing.

Dynamic pricing has been seen at the beginning of COVID-19 pandemic in 2020 when the prices of facemasks and hand sanitisers shot up not necessarily because the costs of input had increased but because of the exponential increase in demand. Other than such exceptions though, dynamic pricing is not for all industries but best suited for hospitality, travel, entertainment, etc. So, we see how the same hotel rooms in temperate regions are sold in the summer at a multifold of their winter rates. Even in winter though, the rates can shoot up if some conference is taking place in a local area. We also see how airlines use highly sophisticated algorithms to determine their fares, depending on several factors. Generally speaking, dynamic pricing tends to apply to the wealthier consumers of goods and services, as they have the capacity and are willing to absorb the differential shocks.

'**Cost plus**' is a typical pricing method that needs special mention in our environment. Ideally, all pricing is actually 'cost plus' in some way, shape of form. Here, the business determines the cost of its product and then adds a mark-up to set a price. A business can, almost arbitrarily, decide to mark-up the cost by, say, thirty per cent. Now this can be simple but it is exactly the simplicity that can cause strategic pricing errors if other factors are not taken into consideration. For instance, at the thirty per cent mark-up mentioned as an example, you could either lose opportunities or kill opportunities for yourself. You lose opportunities if at that mark-up your product is priced below or at the same rate as a competitor's whose product don't offer as much recognised value. On the other hand, you could kill opportunities for yourself because you have over-priced your products in relation to similar and alternative products. The point is, for cost plus pricing method to work well, it has to take other factors into consideration over and beyond your cost and some desired margin.

Every entrepreneur must be clear about the exact value they are providing. Value is not about our personal sentiments and opinions. Rather, it is about what the customer accepts as solving some problem or providing some convenience. Even when we think ahead of the customer and offer some otherwise 'futuristic' solutions or conveniences, the customer ultimately has to see value in the product and accept same at a price that is profitable to us. But providing value to a customer comes at a cost to a business. And since the objective of a business is to deliver the value at a profit, the entrepreneur must not only be meticulous and detailed but also fair in costing their goods and services. Similarly, the entrepreneur should be wise and strategic in pricing their products. If our pricing is above what the market is willing and able to afford, we risk not getting any or only little patronage. On the other hand, if our pricing is below our cost, we may make a lot of sales but would ultimately lose money and perhaps go bankrupt unless we inject fresh funds into the business and/or reprice our products.

18.0 Regulatory Compliance

Many entrepreneurs consider regulatory compliance as an irritant and a business responsibility to avoid. Unfortunately, this is wrong and unwise and the entrepreneur that wishes to succeed in the long run must do away with that thinking. On the contrary, complying with regulations will actually enhance your chances of success.

What is regulatory compliance? A regulatory *requirement* is a rule or law that is legislated or adopted by an appropriate tier of government or responsible agency, which creates a legal obligation on a specific or a range of issues for business organisations. Some regulations may apply to only businesses in a particular location or industry whilst other regulations might apply to all businesses in general within a national jurisdiction. Depending on what you do, certain regulations by other countries or international bodies can also apply to you. A regulatory *compliance*, therefore, refers to the obedience of a business organisation to all legally enforceable rules.

What are the benefits of complying with regulations? The first benefit of complying with regulations is that you and your business get to be on the right side of the law. The business doesn't get to pay fines and damages or suffer through gruelling litigation processes. These help to sharpen your focus by avoiding distractions and saving money, time and effort for the business. In addition, simply being in the basket of regulation gives you and your business the opportunity to engage with authorities formally and socially on regulatory improvements that may help businesses in your area, industry or the country at large. If you are not in the basket, you will neither have the formal platform nor the moral basis to engage with the authorities. If anything, you will be like a mouse that a cat is looking for!

In the year that just passed, an international organisation, in partnership with a local representative, developed a program to help to support micro, small and medium enterprises ('MSMEs') in some states of the federation. The support included a business training program for the owners and management of the MSMEs as well as the provision of grant. Obviously, the international organisation and its local representative had a set of criteria to allow for intelligent selection of qualifying MSMEs. Needless to say, only MSMEs that operate with reasonable measure of formality were successfully shortlisted and are currently enjoying a free business training and will stand a good chance of getting a financial support.

Regulations and Regulators: In Nigeria, there are regulations that may be enacted by local, state or federal governments. It is necessary that an entrepreneur not only familiarises themselves but also be fully conversant with all regulations that affect their business, their staff, their goods and services as well as themselves. Some of these regulations include business name registration or incorporation, pension payments, income tax payments, business premises, purchase and the use of some types of equipment, the production and distribution of certain goods, environmental management, handling dangerous goods, etc.

In addition to being conversant with regulations, the entrepreneur should also be aware of the specific government agencies that they will be dealing with on each issue. These include Corporate Affairs Commission ('CAC'), Federal Inland Revenue Service ('FIRS'), Nigeria Social Insurance Trust Fund ('NSITF'), National Agency for Food and Drug Administration and Control ('NAFDAC'), Department of Petroleum Resource ('DPR'), Nigerian Nuclear Regulatory Authority ('NNRA'), Standards Organization of Nigeria ('SON'), Central Bank of Nigeria ('CBN'), Industrial Training Fund ('ITF'), Pension Commission ('PenCom'), Nigeria Customs Services, state Ministries of Commerce, etc.

The Professionals: The one or two stop 'shops' you must liaise with to establish which regulations are applicable to your business and which government agencies are responsible for those regulations are your accountant and your lawyer. These two professionals will help to put you through the regulations to do with your interested business. Ensure that you understand the compliance procedures as well as the cost implications of each regulation. There might be one-off payments for some permits and authorisations whilst others might attract regular payments, depending on your turnover, staff strength or some other variables. Having a full picture of all such charges is critical to establishing your cost structure as well as developing a pricing model.

Business Associations: In addition to government agencies, voluntary business associations can formulate policies aimed at enhancing their common interests. The entrepreneur is encouraged to participate in such associations for many of the same reasons for complying with government regulations. But while the policies of the associations might not be legally binding on the entrepreneur and their business, being a part of such associations gives you a platform to solve certain problems and seize opportunities. For instance, governments and their agencies are known to graciously listen to such associations for input when considering the enactment or amendment of certain laws. Being a participant in such associations, therefore, provides opportunities to make your input. For as long as the policies of the associations do not contravene government regulations, you can positively consider complying with them.

Complying with regulations is crucial not only in giving us the legitimacy we require to operate our businesses, but also in providing the moral platform we need to be able to engage authorities in matters that affect our businesses.

How to be Regulatory-Compliant

Regulatory compliance is a union of processes, human actions and technology. For instance, the processes of obtaining licenses, approvals, etc. must be known and understood; Individuals and functional units should be identified, trained and charged with the responsibility of doing what needs to be done timely in order for the organisation to be and remain regulatory-compliant. Similarly, technology should be deployed, as much as is possible, to help to remain on the right side of the law. Our computers, phones and their applications can remind us when certain actions should be initiated to ensure that approvals and renewals are obtained timely whilst certain processes can be automated. The schematic diagram below shows a possible regulatory compliance dynamics.

Some of the specific measures an entrepreneur can take to ensure regulatory compliance are:

Start with the right mindset and develop the right culture: In everything that is important, we always must start with the right mindset. In this case, the entrepreneur is required completely and without any 'ifs and buts' resolve to comply always with legally enforceable regulations. Beyond this personal resolve, the entrepreneur should develop and entrench the culture of compliance with the laws in their business. There shouldn't be any alternative discussions on it. It must be clear to everyone that as a matter of policy, all regulations have to always be complied with. Simple.

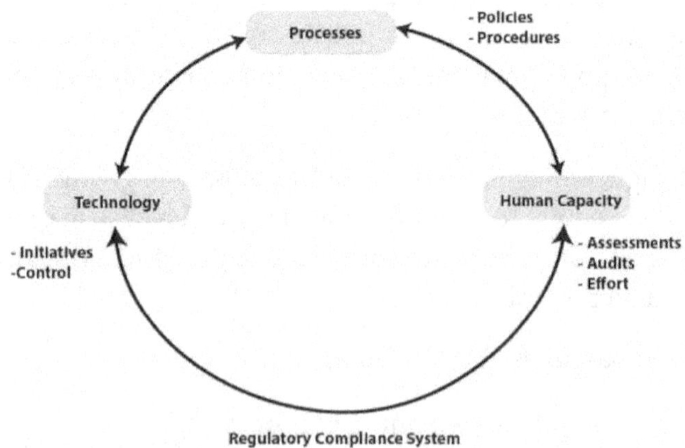

Figure 18.1: Regulatory compliance system
(© Musbahu El Yakub)

Educate your staff on regulatory compliance: *Several years ago, I had the privilege of driving a highly successful, senior and elderly person in my official car to attend a function in the evening. On the way, we were stopped by a team of police officers on traffic beat. They asked for the vehicle documents, which I promptly made available. Unbeknownst to me, one of the documents had expired. It was a little embarrassing as I extricated myself from the situation whilst my passenger said nothing. After leaving the scene, the passenger sternly said to me, 'Musbahu, don't ever allow yourself to get into such situations!' By the bye, it is probably twenty years now and no such documents have, again, ever expired on my hands before they are renewed. Partly, I resolved to renew all vehicle documents at the same time, thereby eliminating the need to monitor each individually.*

Teach your staff to ensure full compliance with all regulations. Make it clear that where staff individually break rules or laws, they will be made to bear any financial consequence that comes with it.

Conduct a regulatory mapping/audit: Once it is adopted as a policy of the organisation always to comply with regulations, the next thing is to conduct a mapping exercise in which all applicable laws are identified. As mentioned in the first part of this series, the good starting point for this are with your Lawyers and Accountants. Working with these professionals will help you to establish which regulations apply to your business, how to meet each, how often you must meet up with the regulatory requirement and any costs associated with that. This exercise should be conducted regularly to ensure that you and your business remain compliant.

Establish a compliance process: After establishing which regulations are applicable to your business, the next challenge is to establish policies and procedures about complying with each requirement. For instance, knowing when a particular permit will expire and the lead time of processing its renewal, you can establish when the renewal process must be initiated to ensure that it is obtained before the current one expires. This might include a user or responsible department initiating the process two months before the current permit expires. Wherever possible, technology should be used to alert and prompt the renewal process. This exercise also involves understanding what the renewal process involves. Is a formal application required? Is there any payment to be made? If a payment is involved, what determines the amount due? How and when will the payment be effected? Etc. Leverage on technology as much as is possible and document the compliance policies and processes. Equally importantly, all documents, soft and hard copies, should be protected.

Designate a compliance champion(s): Depending on what you do and the size of your business, you may need a compliance champion or champions. These may be the CEO or any staff for that matter. Whoever this champion might be, they must be aware of all the regulatory requirements. They should have a system and process of ensuring compliance. And equally importantly, they must be given all the support they need to keep the business compliant of all requirements.

Monitor any changes: Often, Regulators do change the laws. It could be at annual budgets of the federation or a state. It could be at any point by an Agency responsible for granting some permit. To keep abreast of changes, you should be monitoring developments in the economy and society, as well as have a relationship with the regulators.

Complying with regulations is very important. We should do whatever is required to be on the right side of the law. If you cannot 'afford' to be regulatory-compliant, you probably shouldn't be in *that* business.

19.0 Making Partnerships Work

We will shortly discuss relationship management. But beyond then, we will now take up how to build and make business partnerships work. For our purposes here, partnership refers to the act of working together with other individuals and organisations for mutual benefit and not the 'legal' form of business entities other than sole proprietorships and limited liability companies. We will use the term interchangeably with 'collaboration'.

Just a century back into our history, most African societies were highly communal. From working together on farms to going on joint hunting expeditions, Africans had a history of working together for survival. Ironically, we haven't seemed to have moved fully to the next level of 'partnering' in ways that will grow us as individuals, business organisations and modern nations.

The legal forms of business partnerships and limited liability companies were actually conceptualised to not only allow for but also encourage collaboration between individuals and organisations in creating business entities. But beyond the formality of partnering to create an appropriate business vehicle, collaborating with others is key not only to the success of a business but also its long-term success and growth.

We frequently see small scale as well as bigtime businessmen and women in other parts of the world working together to achieve certain business objectives. Bill Gates and the late Steve Jobs running Microsoft and Apple respectively were rivals that competed heavily against each other. Yet, in 1997, Bill Gates invested $150 million in a then struggling Apple, saving the company from bankruptcy. (In return for the investment, Apple also dropped a legal suit against Microsoft.) The point is, even 'bitter' competitors can work together for individual or common goals.

For me, a decidedly important question is, therefore, how can Africans improve their capacity and willingness to partner together in business as a matter of routine rather than exceptions?

What is Partnering? Partnering together in our context here refers to individual businessmen and women and business entities working in sync, formally or informally, to achieve business goals. This includes two or more individuals coming together to start a business or two competing businesses working with each other to promote some legitimate interests. It may be individual artisans forming a cooperative society or a lead agricultural firm working with scores of farmers or farming businesses to achieve individual and collective objectives. The spectrum of possibilities is truly wide and deep.

The Benefits of Partnering: As mentioned above, collaboration offers a whole spectrum of possible working relationships that can be designed by individuals and organisations and it has several benefits, such as:

- **Pooling resources together:** Collaborating entities can pool all sorts of resources to achieve identified objectives. These resources could include, time, finances, expertise, rights, capital equipment, contacts, etc. The availability of the resources is what may help to create or seize opportunities for the entities.

- **Increase efficiency and effectiveness:** Collaborating entities can jointly increase their mutual efficiency and effectiveness by working together.

- **Risk management:** Partnering entities can work together in ways that help them to manage various risks.

- **Other benefits** include the optimum use of facilities, human capital development, etc.

Elements of Collaboration: There are just two elements of partnering together, Objectives and Resources. Individual collaborating entities must be clear of exactly their objectives in the relationship.

Sometimes all the objectives are known to all the entities, but other times only individual partners might know the full details of the objectives from their perspective. The latter is as fine as the former as long as a partner does not in any way hurt the other entity or entities in pursuit of their latent objective(s).

The other element is resources. You go into collaboration knowing well what resources you are able to provide and also what resources other entity or entities are also providing. You do not go collaborating with an entity that doesn't offer any value.

A third factor but which doesn't warrant being a full element is legality. Most partnering agreements should be legally documented, as we shall see later. But at least a few will be understandings that may not be legally enforceable. Where legality and enforcement are possible or appropriate, an agreement should be documented. Where it is not necessary or enforceable, however, other factors, such as the character of individuals, track record or organisations, etc. should be checked to ensure that entities will respect understandings even if there is not any formal, legally enforceable agreements.

Partnership Philosophy: To develop and sustain successful partnerships, you and your organisation must have the right partnership philosophy. These include:

- **Mean well:** You must mean well to your partners. This includes being fair, transparent, honest and having their back.

- **Think long-term:** You must think long-term in developing relationship with your partners. You have to see the relationship beyond the vagaries of individual transactions.

- **Create opportunities:** Look out for and create opportunities for your partners beyond your agreement or transactions with them.

Circles of Partnerships: As an individual or corporate entity, you can generally collaborate with other individual or corporate investors, suppliers, customers, etc. You could also form strategic partnerships with individuals and organisations even if you do not have any current business *per se* with them. The possible circles of relationships are a whole maze that must be developed, nurtured and navigated deliberately.

We have so far defined the concept of business collaboration and brought out its benefits, elements and philosophy. Next, we will conclude on the circles of partnerships that we introduced and discuss some principles and practices of successful business partnering.

Circles of Relationships: Like the human individual, a business entity belongs to several relationship circles. Typically, there would be investors, creditors, suppliers, employees, customers, regulators, etc. Your peculiar situation and circumstances as well as your type of business will determine what relationships carry what weight. Regardless of the type and weight of each relationship, the challenge in business collaboration is to create, nurture and grow them into successful, mutually rewarding partnerships.

Types of Collaborations: Generally speaking, there are two types of collaborations, internal and external. Internal collaborations are when individuals and groups across the same business organisation 'partner' together in respect of their day-to-day operations as well as on long-term projects. This is essentially the teamwork we expect to see in organisations as a minimum. External collaborations refer to the various forms of corporate partnerships that are aimed at achieving certain objectives between two or more business organisations. These include *Ecosystems, Portfolio, Alliance, Co-opetition, Network,* etc.

Practices of Business Collaboration: We have mentioned partnering philosophies as, meaning well, thinking long-term and creating opportunities for partners. These must always be the basis of your thoughts and actions. They are the foundations for wise business collaborative practices, such as:

- **Identify Key Relationships:** Your first challenge is to identify key persons and organisations that you will need to partner with. The individuals might, for instance, be high net-worth persons that can provide equity funding or those highly placed in the society that can be mentors or helpful in opening doors for you. There could also be organisations that you will need to build healthy, mutually rewarding partnerships with. As mentioned, these could include your corporate customers, suppliers, creditors, regulators, etc.

  Obviously, organisations are made up of individuals. So, key components of developing partnerships with organisations are those persons that run the organisations or have a bearing on them. These could be junior employees, middle-level employees, senior employees, external directors, etc. Similarly, you should identify both those that have influence at the moment and those that will grow in the future to have influence. Develop good relationships with all.

- **Engage:** The moment you identify individuals and organisations that you will need to partner with now or will be 'handy' in the future, begin to positively engage with them. As we always mention though, you must not be fixated on your interests only, but should also look out for the interests of the collaborating partner. The moment you do away with your zero-sum mindset and begin to look at things and issues from the perspectives of the partner(s), it will become easy to come up with ideas and solutions that propel all partners forward.

- **Add-Value:** Amongst the elements of business partnering, we mentioned that you should be able to put resources on the table. But beyond just the 'resources' you may be able to commit, the ultimate objective of your partner is that you are able to add value in the relationship. Think about it, the people we are most attached to are those that add value in our lives. We run to them in good and bad times. That is the basis for collaborative success, either for individuals or organisations.

  Think carefully and deliberately of exactly the value you can add in each attempt at collaboration. Clearly, each relationship is different and, therefore, the demands, expectations and efforts will, likewise, be different.

- **Be Reliable:** Trust is one of the pillars on which all successful partnerships are built. Never commit to what you will not be able to deliver and you must always deliver on what you commit to.

  Recently, I was involved in the negotiations between an organisation and a potential client. At a stage, the organisation offered to provide some resources to the client 'free'. Unfortunately, when the financials were agreed to, the actual cost of the 'free' resources amounted to a larger than projected percentage of the net profit to be earned.

  Even though there are times when you can legitimately ask for renegotiations, this wasn't such a case. It was an error in the handling of the negotiations by the organisation. Consequently,

I insisted that the organisation must fulfil that condition without even raising it up with the client, as bringing up the issue will not only lead to questions about their technical competence but also their integrity. I advised that they should learn from the mistake and, in fact, be grateful that they were still making decent money from the transaction.

Being reliable is about being technically competent, trustworthy, looking out for mutual interests and thinking long-term.

- **Institutionalisation:** Obviously, some relationships are best managed by senior executives. However, it is not sufficient that only some senior staff are bought in the collaboration effort. Middle-level staff and even junior operatives must be sufficiently trained to appreciate the collaborative philosophy and practices of the organisation. Often as we see, junior operators and middle-level staff can help or mar the reputation of organisations with their acts of omissions and/or commission. Such internal collaborations should engender a culture within the organisation. It is also applicable externally by partnering organisations jointly training their staff, deploying technology to enhance their collaboration, etc.

Wise collaborative practices will help the entrepreneur and their business immensely. They should be deliberate, well thought-out, practical, farsighted and entrenched within an organisation.

20.0 Creativity and Innovation

Business success is dependent on the ability of an entrepreneur to offer products (goods and services) to their customers. Beyond that, the products must trigger, meet or surpass the expectations of the customers. In making available the products and meeting their expectations, the entrepreneur might, often, necessarily need to differentiate their offerings in some way(s). Being able to differentiate your processes, systems, products, operational models, etc. in ways that engender success is significantly related to your capacity for creativity and innovation, which will be our subject now.

What is Creativity? This refers to the capacity of an individual, a team or organisation to conceptualise new imaginations, possibilities, ideas, etc. Creativity could be about the development of entirely new or only partially new ideas.

The creative process is usually imaginative through thinking something new that is not, usually, quantifiable. Creativity comes with little or no incremental financial costs or risks. It is about the intellectual development of some fully original or significantly modified idea. Typically, creativity revolves around inspiration, thought and knowledge that may unleash a great potential for changes in a field or related/unrelated array of fields.

What is Innovation? Innovation is the act or process of converting a creative thought or idea into something that is practical. It is about development and implementation of new ideas, which ultimately create some desired value.

The process of innovation usually leads to the eventual introduction of something new and quantifiable and may come with financial costs and attendant risks. Innovation can lead to the development of new technology, new products, improve existing technologies, existing products, new methods and processes, improve existing methods and processes, full or partial system developments, etc. Innovation revolves around turning a creative idea into a practical, useable and viable solution.

Even as we strive to establish an academic and industrial distinction between creativity and innovation though, we also must realise the causal and dynamic link between the two, as shown below:

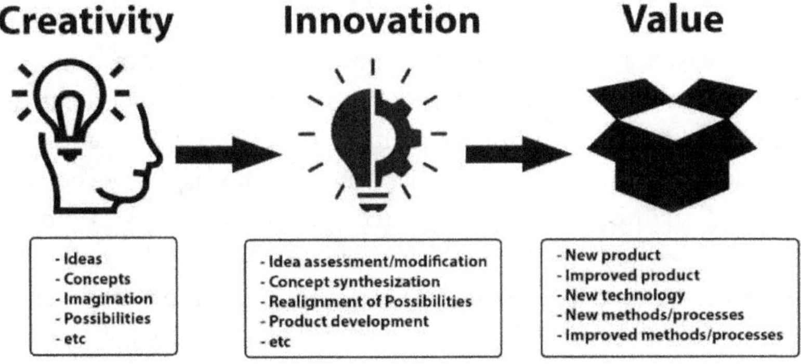

Figure 20.1: Creativity, innovation and value link
(© Musbahu El Yakub)

The Benefits of Creativity and Innovation: Globalisation and technology have widened and deepened opportunities for businesses of all sizes and in all crannies of the planet. But those two variables have, on the other hand, also helped in crowding the marketplace, resulting in increased competition. Consequently, in whichever sphere you operate, you will need your creative and innovative hats perpetually on. Creativity and innovation make it possible for entrepreneurs to conceive and/or seize opportunities in ways that offer them advantages. Creativity and innovation help to bring out more value at lower operational costs with attendant benefits to customers. Creativity and innovation make it possible for us to open up entirely new business models and even industries.

The Scope of Creativity and Innovation: The scope of the applicability of creativity and innovation in every business is wholly.

From commercial ideas, naming the business, product ideas and product names, development of logo for the business and product to raising funds from investors and creditors, capital structure, working capital management strategy, product promotions, production and logistics operations, market research, penetration and development, human capital management, business modelling and relationship management, etc. There, simply, are vast opportunity points for being creative and innovative.

Both creativity and innovation can be incremental or radical. But more often than not, entrepreneurs and their managers focus on making incremental improvements and do derive contentment and limited results therefrom. In other situations, however, it is only radical improvements that can create the kind of ideas and solutions required to take a business to the big league. The entrepreneur and their team should always be on the alert for such ideas and solutions, which, interestingly, can be inspired at the oddest of times and situations.

Who Should be Involved in Creative and Innovative Processes?

A lot of people assume that individuals and organisations are either creative and/or innovative or not. Thankfully, this is not entirely correct as both individuals and organisations can develop and grow their creative and innovative capacities. We will discuss how that can be done. For now, what is important is to realise that every individual in a system can come up with creative ideas and/or innovative solutions. But to build and enhance the chances of developing these capacities, there must be a channel and formal, even if fluid, process of nurturing, bringing out and capturing these activities and the results. It goes without saying, therefore, that all your people should be trained on how to be engaged in coming up with ideas and solutions, as well as rewarded for all that.

Each individual in your system is engaged in certain activities and engagements with other people. Your pool driver can come up with ideas on how to save fuel costs on your fleet of vehicles. Your production headman can come up with an idea and your production engineer can come up with a solution on how to eliminate raw material wastages at a particular production stage. Your accountant can come up with a brilliant metric assessment system, etc. The point is, every individual or team should be encouraged, engaged and incentivised to be creative and innovative.

So far, we have introduced what creativity and innovation (C & I) are in business, their benefits, scope and who should be involved in ideas generation. Success is dependent on the ability of an entrepreneur and their business to be creative and innovative in delivering value.

How to Develop a Business Culture of C & I

There are three elements of C & I, viz: people, systems, rewards and incentivisation. Each of these need to be incorporated into a whole that makes it possible, easy and beneficial to be creative and innovative.

People Elements: Your people are the most important resource you have. We assume here that you have been diligent in your staff engagement processes to get the best people that you need. But beyond getting the best people, you will also need to keep them results-driven, focussed and committed to coming up with brilliant and workable ideas that will put and keep your business ahead. This will require that you train them to understand, appreciate and be excited being creative and innovative. Expose your people to the wide scope of creativity to innovation in the various ways that can add value to your operations.

Systemic Elements: The system you create must be not only be receptive to but also encourage acts of creativity and innovation by your people. Train your people and make it easy for them to be alert, observant, curious and thoughtful. Suggestions, no matter how 'ridiculous' should be listened to and only killed on the basis of superior arguments.

Incentivisation Factors: To succeed in business, you need a continuous flow of ideas. Out of several ideas, many might either not be workable and as many others might not deliver the results expected. But if just a few ideas, depending on their profundity, add value as expected, they can significantly enhance the fortunes of an organisation. People can be motivated to act in desirable ways by doing the right things. The Apples, Samsungs, General Electrics, etc. of this world are only as successful as they are able to keep ahead of their competitors through continuous C & I.

Incentivise the efforts, not only the results, of your people to come up with creative and innovative ideas. It is important to encourage the efforts which should be rewarded in wise ways whilst also rewarding the results that are ultimately achieved.

Specifically, there are several ways of coming up with ideas in a business organisation. These include, but are, obviously, not limited to:

Seek continuous improvement: Everyone in your organisation must continuously be hungry for new ideas to improve systems, processes, products, experiences, etc. It is about always asking questions, turning things and ideas on their head. Just never be satisfied with what you have.

Encourage individuality: Each person is different and unique. Some perform best in the mornings whilst others are nighthawks. Some like to be alone at their best moments whilst others like to be with others. Within the limits of legitimacy and operationality, encourage whatever it is that brings out the best of your people.

Encourage teamwork: Even as individuals are encouraged and allowed to come out with their best in the ways that best works for them, they, however, must respect the spirit of working together with others. Often, our ideas will only be complete by sounding it out to others who can help to refine them.

Create silent spaces: We have earlier recognised that some people come up with their best in what others would consider rowdy situations. However, there are others who need silence to process, articulate and put their thoughts together. Create a silent space where people that need to can go think through their ideas. Others might like to take a walk perhaps to a nearby coffee shop where they will be alone or with a colleague. Allow them! The point is let people be able to detect their best creative moments and seize them.

Reward out-of-the-box thinking: Positive reinforcement is quite often a good way to encourage desired behaviours. Rewarding people to motivate them further is often cheaper than we think of it. Sometimes it is a gift from the boss who just returned from a foreign trip that will do the trick. It could be a corporate gift that means something to the staff. It could also be a public commendation or formal letter of appreciation. What is important is that you understand your people and come up with what they value.

Conduct stand-up meetings: Our energy levels are different between when we are seated and when we are standing. Some short meetings can be conducted when people are standing. The enthusiasm soars in such situations and the thinking process of people is facilitated. The ability of people to 'think on their feet' helps them solve to problems faster in other situations.

Observe nature: As brilliant as we may be, we are great copycats from what is naturally abundant around us. For instance, aeronautical engineers look to nature for inspiration on new ways to make aircrafts lighters and more fuel efficient. So do marine engineers in developing and improving the capacities of ships and submarines. These opportunities of stealing ideas from nature are available in most fields of business and life.

Challenge yourself and your team: The tendency is always for us to take things easy. We cannot be creative or innovative by taking things easy. To avoid complacency and resting on our oars, we should always consciously challenge ourselves into coming up with both mild, at least, and radical changes, preferably, in what we do and how we do them.

Creativity and innovation are fundamental to the renewal, growth and success of every business. The entrepreneur must engender and sustain the two activities if they are to be able to do things differently and better than the competition.

21.0 Contract Negotiations

Most entrepreneurs are clear that making sales is critical to the short-term survival and long-term success of their business. Sales could be made by selling simple commodities like soaps, honey, etc. by a business. But more often, sales are achieved through a 'contract' that includes the components of both goods and services as well as some other legitimate 'terms and conditions'. For instance, a poultry farm may enter into an agreement to supply a certain weight of dressed chicken to a wholesale outlet. Other terms, than the total weight of all the chicken to be delivered, might include the minimum weight of each chicken, the day of the month for the delivery and the type of packaging as well as the labelling on each package, etc.

Unfortunately, many entrepreneurs, in a hurry and excitement to clinch a deal, tend to just focus on pricing. They end up accepting other terms even if they are far-fetched or will come at an additional cost to them that may make the complete deal unattractive. Some other times, inexperienced and unwise entrepreneurs knowingly accept terms that they do not have the sincere intention of fulfilling. They just assume that once they get the business, the client must accept and live with what they ultimately deliver. The consequence of this includes cost overruns, likely delays, poor or incomplete deliveries and failures that make the client dissatisfied at the end of the transaction.

The failure to make final deliveries in *full* compliance with *all* the terms agreed to with a client has several negative immediate and long-term repercussions on the entrepreneur and their business. In the first instance and at the minimum, the client is disappointed. The failure could also hurt the client tremendously that they could successfully sue you and claim damages. Besides having the right to do so, a client may likely never again patronise you. Beyond that, they may strongly advise their business associates against patronising you.

Not meeting with what you promised your customer, whether your agreement was documented or not and whether there was an initial formal intent to seek legal remedy or not, is a failure that must be averted.

To avoid the likelihood of such failures, it is essential that entrepreneurs consider each transaction as a contract, irrespective of scope and value. This is important, so that the entrepreneur can take the deal seriously and do what needs to be done in a way that makes the transaction profitable and the relationship mutually rewarding. When customers are happy, they not only give us repeat businesses, but they also recommend us to their family, friends and associates.

How do we inspire a farsighted approach in, and a relationship-biased contract-mindset of, handling our transactions in our businesses?

Think of the lifetime value of customers: The way to take all the terms and conditions of a transaction seriously is to appreciate the potential lifetime value of the customer. First, realise that each fully completed transaction helps to build a lasting and mutually rewarding relationship with a customer. A lasting and mutually beneficial relationship with a customer means the value you stand to gain over the coming years is worth more than the costs of the relationship. Similarly, you should appreciate that there is no amount you can benefit from the customer on a one-off basis that will be worth a sustained relationship and the benefits of the recommendations that they are likely to make to others on your behalf if they are happy with you. Therefore, look beyond one-off benefits and instead seek to build a relationship by doing the right things.

Consider each transaction as a binding contract: Seeking to build a relationship with a customer means you have to take each transaction as a contract irrespective of value and details. As mentioned earlier and also discussed in our previous series 'Keep Your

Word', you must always strive to be true to your word. Regardless of the levels of formality and documentations made in respect of the transaction, ensure that your word remains your bond. Simply put, take each commitment you make as sacrosanct.

A special attention that needs to be drawn here is that as an entrepreneur, you should strive always to do what is right regardless of the general proclivity to do wrong in our society in the misguided belief that 'you will get away with it'. What we need to realise is that we actually never get away with wrong-doing. We either pay a price now or later. We may or may not discern that a price we pay has to do with a specific wrong-doing. But there is always a price to be paid for each wrong-doing in our lives. Somehow, somewhere. Always.

Understand what a contract is: In its simplest form, a contract is a promise that is enforceable by law. For instance, it may be a promise to deliver a product of some quality by a certain date. In its more comprehensive form, a contract is a binding agreement that defines and governs the rights and duties of the parties to the agreement.

For our purposes here, any commitment the entrepreneur makes and agrees to should be viewed as a contract regardless of whether or not it is enforceable by law. The point is for the entrepreneur to take the highest moral and professional standards of ensuring that their word, explicit or implied, is their bond. This mindset is important if the entrepreneur is to be able to take each business discussion seriously.

The sincere willingness and ability to meet all contractual commitments irrespective of details is crucial to the long-term success of every human being and business.

To this point we have posited that most entrepreneurs are reasonably clear about the importance of sales in the short-term survival and long-term success of their business. We brought out the need to have a long-term perspective in developing customer relation-ships as well as some of the ways an entrepreneur can inspire a farsighted, relationship-biased and contract-mindset for handling business transactions in themselves and their business. We will now take up some of the building blocks of living that purpose.

Think long-term: Each transaction, no matter how transient it might seem, has the possibility of creating or ruining future business opportunities. When customers interact with us, their experience, pleasant or not, has the tendency to last. Therefore, if we appreciate the possible long-term consequences of each inter-action, we will be more inclined to doing what is right, thereby giving our customers positive experiences. This, in return, will make it possible for them to either come back or refer others to us. Thinking long-term makes us moderate and sharpen our behav-iours.

Be willing to pass a business opportunity: Sometimes, the en-trepreneur is called upon by a client to do something that the entrepreneur cannot or should not do. In the former category are the situations in which the entrepreneur does not have the compe-tence or required resources to do what the customer demands. If you cannot on technical grounds do what is demanded of you and cannot work with other entrepreneurs to get the job done as ex-pected, you should back down on the deal. Similarly, if the customer asks or in any way implies that you should do something that is either morally wrong or outrightly illegal, let the deal pass!

One of the things that entrepreneurs in our environment find difficult to do is to pass on deals even when there is a rationale for doing just that. But the rules of thumb are: If you cannot deliver fully and satis-factorily, let the deal pass; if a client expects you to serve them by getting on the wrong side of the law, let the deal pass!

If we ever have to fall short, it must not be because we lack the re-sources or competence or for failure to fully apply ourselves. It should only be because of extraneous issues outside of our control.

Learn to negotiate: Running a business entails having to often negotiate with others. Whatever may be the subject, the entrepreneur should take negotiations seriously. This means you must be thoughtful to everything you say and commit to. If in the course of some negotiations you are not able to immediately decide on a specific request by your customer, you can always ask to have more time to consider and revert. Just remember that as soon as you commit to do something, it is binding on you to discharge it. If after your agreement, however, legitimate and innocent justifications arise that necessitate a reconsideration of terms, then you can, in the most responsible way, call for a review. In such situations, you must conduct yourself fairly and honourably.

Understand your business: To make your negotiations successful and minimise the risks for having to call for reviews later, you need to understand your business well. For instance, what is your cost structure? What are the realistic delivery timelines based on empirical experiences, etc? Understanding your business, industry standards and practices are important in working out profitable deals with your customers.

Be clear about all terms: The usual terms that get discussed in business deals include pricing, quality standards, measures, packaging, labelling, delivery schedule(s), etc. It is compulsory that an entrepreneur is conversant with the common terms of trade in their business. Where a customer requires certain shifts from the usual terms, you should not shy away from discussing any likely cost implications and, therefore, price changes.

In our environment, it is common that entrepreneurs often agree to all other terms once the pricing seem potentially profitable, unalive to the reality that the other terms may be unrealistic or can significantly erode their margins. This is foolish and each entrepreneur must extricate themselves from this practice.

Always endeavour to document the details of your agreement. Where it is considered not necessary to document an agreement, the least you should do is to take a personal note. In the heat of daily vagaries, many of us innocently forget some of what might have been agreed to. A personal note can refreshen our memory.

Make everything simple: *My first and second degrees are in Nuclear Physics and I learnt something very interesting in the way the physics community of scientists informally 'assesses' their members. Obviously, every worthy physicist must generally be incisive in their thinking and erudite with their mathematics. However, the best physicists are not considered to be the ones that can introduce or work out complex concepts and mathematics. Rather, the best physicists are those that can simplify the most difficult concepts and mathematics in a way that even a non-physicist can understand.*

Making difficult things seem elementary is one of the ways otherwise formidable challenges can be made popular, exciting and achievable. In negotiating and managing business transactions, simplifying things makes them unambiguous, allowing you to achieve your goals and strengthen your relationships.

It is fundamental to the success of our businesses that we approach and handle each current transaction with the understanding that it has a link to the prospects of future opportunities. A way to successfully navigate the approach is to have a long-term perspective of each transaction and handle it appropriately.

Chapter 4

"Do the best you can until you know better. Then when you understand better, do better." - Maya Angelou

22.0 Getting Things Done

We have so far discussed several entrepreneurial issues and built them from the ground up. We have discussed mindset, business planning, funding, staffing, etc. We will now discuss one common factor that binds all successful entrepreneurs together: Getting things done.

Jack Welch, the former Chief Executive of General Electric ('GE'), was one of the greatest corporate executives of modern times. He succeeded in sharpening the focus of the behemoth GE is. He made it a highly responsive and competitive giant, raising its market capitalisation from $14 billion to about $400 billion over a period of twenty years and making it the then most valuable company in the world. Mr. Welch was passionate about 'execution' or getting things done.

Nothing happens unless you do something. In fact, if you don't do something, it is bad stuff that usually happens. Remember entropy and Murphy's 'law'? So, how do you develop the personal discipline of getting things done?

Always start within your mind: Everything we do or don't actually starts from our minds, either consciously or subconsciously. The most successful people in all trades and professions are always conscious of what they are doing. Fundamentally, they have internalised to 'do something' about anything important that comes their way. They may not like what is happening, but they will always consider the issue seriously and then take appropriate action.

Condition your mind and your body to take appropriate action anytime anything comes up.

Be very comfortable solving problems: Many of us wish for a world and a business life in which there are no problems. Well, sorry, the world doesn't operate that way. Our best plans are challenged and we must always be ready to adjust *what is happening* to *what we want to see happen*. The richest man on the African continent, Alhaji Aliko Dangote, said something like, when he wakes up every morning, he gets ready to solve problems (that has to do with seizing some opportunity). That is the life of success. It is a life of 'getting things done'.

Create a routine: The most successful and the least successful people in the world all have twenty-four hours in a day. But the former are highly effective and efficient in the use of their time.

In this our information age, it is quite easy to get distracted with phones and computers, as well as television and even friends. To succeed, you must create a routine in your life. You should plan your day, making your 'to-do list' usually the night before. Start your day early. The extra hour in the mornings you are able to create will add up substantially in the course of the years.

Prioritise and plan: There are always several things to do. But the most successful people are able to choose what will add the most value in their lives and professions and accord them required priority. To prioritise effectively, you must be able to distinguish between what is urgent and what is important and act wisely.

Some people are 'morning people' and some others are 'evening people', meaning that they tend to be most productive in the mornings or evenings, respectively. Whatever type of person you may be, you should try to discharge the most important tasks at the times of the day you are most productive. Set out times to check and respond to your mails, conduct your meetings, exercise, take breaks, exercise, etc. And another quality time you must set out is your 'quiet time' during which you can be alone to review important documents, think through far-reaching issues, etc.

Set deadlines: All tasks, especially the most compelling ones, must have deadlines. Never leave tasks open-ended. Setting deadlines helps you to overcome procrastination. It also makes you accountable to yourself irrespective of third-party interests in the tasks at hand. In setting deadlines, try to push yourself but also be realistic.

Focus: A crucial dimension of effective execution is 'focus'. Forget all the calls for 'multi-tasking' by many who probably derive their satisfaction just from doing many things at the same time irrespective of the ultimate results they deliver. Rather, learn to focus on the important things you are trying to do. Think through them very well; go through intelligent problem-solving process; make your decisions and then begin to take action. Focus eliminates noise and distractions, and it enhances the quality of your decisions.

Add 'no' to your dictionary: Irrespective of what we do, there will be all sorts of requests from others. It could be an invitation to attend a meeting, wedding, a cocktail party or for some business favours. Look at all such requests critically and be sure that they are important in the global scheme of what you are doing. If not, do not hesitate to extend a polite but firm 'No'. You need to free your time for other more essential activities.

Reward yourself: In our hyperactive world, it is easy for us to fail to realise our successes. Sometimes, we often benchmark with others and don't take notice of our daily triumphs. This is not just wrong but counterproductive. We should appreciate ourselves and be grateful for our accomplishments not just by being conscious of them but also by giving ourselves legitimate treats.

No matter how good your business plan or how competent you staff may be, you will not achieve anything unless you and your people develop and maintain a culture getting things done timely, effectively and efficiently.

23.0 Prioritisation

We have discussed 'execution' or 'getting things done'. But for us to make a success in our professions and life, we need to get the *right things* done. The only way we can get the right things done is through scrupulous prioritisation.

Prioritisation is the process of deciding the relative order of tasks requiring action to be taken in the pursuit of our legitimate goals. Wise prioritisation helps us to attain greater focus on what we do; enhances productivity and engenders self-confidence. So, how do we prioritise which tasks should take precedence over others?

Have a purpose: Having a purpose in life is the 'Northern star' we all need to help us to guide our thought on the actions that we need to take on everything that comes our way. A purpose is that fundamental reason why we do what we do.

Over time and as we cross different stages in life, our purpose might change. But after a while though, we really must be clear about what we want and what we stand for. A purpose, therefore, is not a destination but a journey on a decided and defined path. Without a sense of purpose, we are unable to set clear goals that take us on a pre-determined path and life itself can lose meaning and direction.

Set your goals: With a path set out by purpose, we need to set the goals we intend to achieve over various and reasonably distant mileposts into the horizon. Our goals are our ideas of a future that we envisage and plan to achieve. Goals can be applied in each sphere of our lives, such as our education, health, career, etc., but they must be in congruence with the chosen purpose. Setting goals is the first step towards making commitments and taking the actions required to reach various strategic milestones on our chosen path.

Build a master list: To achieve our long-term goals, we need to identify our objectives. Objectives are the actionable tasks we need to complete within short timeframes in order to reach a certain goal. Our daily objectives that need to be completed may include responding to mails, meetings with our raw materials' suppliers, making deliveries to some customers, renegotiating an expiring contract with a client, etc.

As mentioned in 'Getting Things Done', we need to plan our days. The way to start off the planning process is to create a 'master list' of 'everything that needs to be done'. The object is to first capture all the tasks that need to be discharged regardless of any ranking yet.

Build an Eisenhower Matrix: It is one thing to create our master list and quite another to prioritise them. The 'Important vs Urgent' matrix was said to be first developed by former United States' President Dwight Eisenhower. The idea is that each task should be classified according to its 'importance' and 'urgency'. 'Important' and 'urgent' tasks should be given the highest priority and, consequently, the most attention immediately. At the other end, 'not urgent'/'not important' tasks are a distraction and should be eliminated from the list entirely.

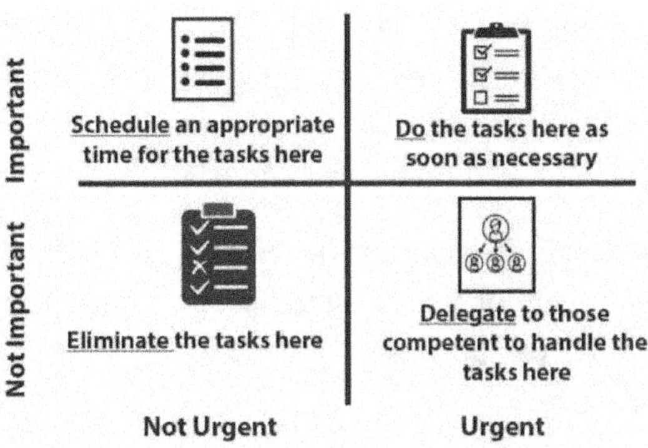

Figure 23.1: Task matrix
(© Musbahu El Yakub)

Apply the 80-20 Rule: A relatively easy way to work out your Eisenhower matrix is by applying a Pareto analysis to the tasks on hand.

Vilfredo Pareto (1848 – 1923) was an Italian economist. Pareto had noticed that 20% of the pea pods in his garden produced 80% of all the peas. He went on to expand this principle to macroeconomics by demonstrating that 20% of the population owned 80% of the wealth in Italy.

There is little scientific proof to this 'principle'. But there seems to be anecdotal evidences in support of the validity of the '80-20 rule', as it has come to be known. It is particularly important in identifying what activities add the most value in what we do. For instance, which twenty of our one hundred customers contribute to our profitability the most, and, therefore, which should we focus and channel our resources on the most?

'Eat that Frog' first! The tactics required to discharge the tasks on hand may differ by person and situation. Regardless though, it is often best we start with the 'difficult' but important tasks. Mark Twain wrote, *"If it's your job to eat a frog, it's best to do it first thing in the morning. And if it's your job to eat two frogs, it's best to eat the biggest one first."* In addition to getting done with a crucial task, 'winning' early in the day motivates us to continue with the other tasks on our list. Alternatively, it could also be wise sometimes to start with some 'easy' tasks just so we clear them away to be able to keep our focus on the 'difficult and important'.

Prioritisation is key to success in everything we do. It creates focus on the important actions we need to take to achieve our objectives and goals and live our purpose.

24.0 Relationship Management

So far, most of the business issues we have discussed, such as staffing, business planning, raising funds, etc., have to do, significantly, with the *technical skills* of the entrepreneur. Unfortunately, as in most professions and careers, so much more emphasis is placed in schools and at work on our technical competence without a corresponding and matching attempt at developing our requisite relationship skills. This is both wrong and counterproductive because in the long run the entrepreneur and their business can suffer tremendously as a result of weak relationship management competency. We will now take up this important life and business factor known as Relationship Management.

Generally speaking, two broad proficiencies are imperative to success in most spheres of our lives, viz: 'technical' and relationship skills. Here, we refer to technical skills as the abilities that we require to perform the intellectual tasks of our jobs. They are our analytical capacities in our specific professions as bankers, engineers, doctors, artists or whatever else. The technical skills of a Cost Accountant, for instance, will be everything to do with their savvy in identifying costs, analysing them and advising how best they can be eliminated or optimised. On the other hand, relationship skills are the totality of our social prowess required to establish, maintain and grow healthy and rewarding relationships with the diverse individuals and groups that we interact with daily. The relationship skills of a Lawyer, for instance, will have everything to do with their ability to engage positively with their colleagues, clients, associates, etc., while also delivering the expected technical results. The fundamentals of relationship management are best understood within the context and scope of the study of emotional intelligence.

It is scientifically established that our emotions precede our thoughts. In addition, our emotions can alter the way our brains normally function and drive our behaviours. And as hard as we might try, we are not always able to leave our emotions at home in the mornings or at the door when we get to work (and vice versa!) Consequently, detecting and managing our emotions and the emotions of others is crucial to achieving desired results. Emotional intelligence is all about our capacity to detect, recognise, understand and manage our emotions as well detect, recognise, understand and manage the emotions of others.

There are four elements of emotional intelligence viz: self-awareness, self-management, social-awareness and relationship management. Working to also improve our emotional intelligence through mastering its composite elements will help us to achieve greater success and faster, too, than focusing entirely on building only our technical aptitudes.

Relationship management is about our interpersonal relationships with everyone we interact with as family, friends, colleagues, customers, etc. Our good relationship management skills are about our abilities to appreciate what other people may be going through and what we can do to enhance their productivity regardless. These skills will make it possible for us to inspire and positively influence others; It will make it possible for us to help others change for the better and grow. Good relationship management is about enhancing our potentials of getting others to willingly do the best they should or can.

The objective of relationship management is for you to enhance your capacity to deliver superlative results, at any given technical skill level, through relating and working with others better. Effective relationship management makes you aware of how best to work with others, thereby enhancing your and others' chances of success. Remember, employers and bosses do not like negative workers no matter how otherwise brilliant they may be. Customers do not like rude and dishonest service providers. Workers do not like toxic, difficult and uncooperative colleagues, etc. The emotionally intelligent individual, on the other hand, can build and nourish healthy and fruitful relationships with others. They can have difficult conversations without hurting the feelings of others. They will always be honest. They will be loyal without being self-seeking. They can resolve conflicts, coach, motivate and guide others.

Obviously, there are various spheres of relationships that encapsulate us. We have to be aware of each, who the stakeholders within each sphere are, their educational levels, biases, interests, etc. Even within the same sphere, individuals do differ in their temperaments, ambitions, insecurities, etc. We should understand each individual and work out how best to manage our relationship with them.

The diagram below typifies simple and static relationship spheres comprising only four groups of stakeholders. Obviously, our relationship universe is so much more dynamic and complex. Thankfully, the principles and methods of building healthy relationships are generally the same for most people in most spheres.

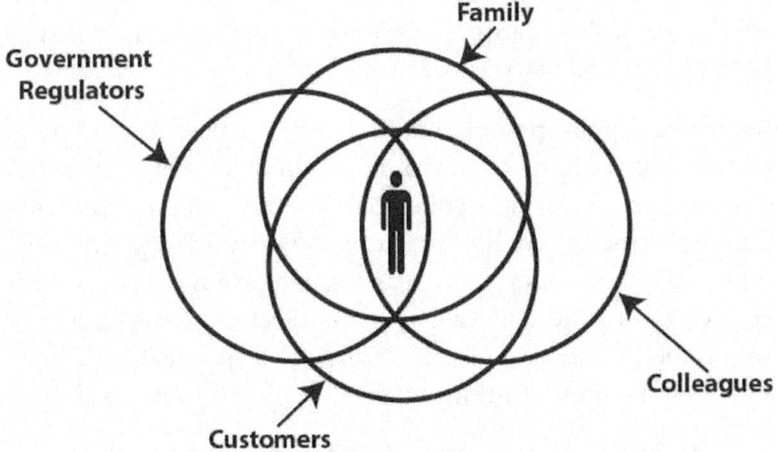

Figure 24.1: Relationship circles
(© Musbahu El Yakub)

So far, we have introduced what Relationship Management is as well as its essence and weight in shaping our successes in life. We also introduced the concept of relationship spheres in which we suggested that we engage with different people in different spheres around us. For instance, we have our families, friends, colleagues, etc. with whom we interact at different times and different spaces.

The people, their requirements and expectations are, at least slightly, dissimilar from one sphere to another. Even within the same sphere, individuals are different with disparate temperaments, motivations and capacities. We have to understand those differences and relate with each sphere and person appropriately. For our purpose here, we are interested in how an entrepreneur can effectively relate with the individuals within their business universe. By business universe, we mean the various spheres composing of colleagues at work, customers, suppliers, professional service providers, such as lawyers, external auditors, etc.

Now we are interested in *how* the entrepreneur can build effective and healthy working relationships with their stakeholders. Even though the people in different spheres may be like chalk and cheese, thankfully, the fundamental principles and practices of building mutually rewarding relationships with them are generally the same. We will try to cover some of these over this as follows:

Be technically competent: The first thing you need to do to stand a chance of creating and developing a meaningful relationship with others is to be technically competent in what you do. Your technical competence may be the reason why you even get to meet some people either as your colleagues, employees or clients. People love those who add value to their lives and your technical competence will make it possible for you to do just that with them. Start from there and continue to develop your technical skills.

Work to build relationships: Good and healthy relationships don't grow on trees! They must be built, nurtured and protected. The way to do it is by deliberately planning and working at it. Make out time for the people in your universe. This would often be a combination of regular phone calls, visits, official and even private support, etc. Whatever it is you are doing with them, be sincerely interested in the persons, their interests, fears, hopes, etc.

Our technical skills will always help us to get opportunities and footholds. They can also help us to get second chances when we mess up. But it is our relationship skills that sustain us over the long run with other people. The easiest way to building and sustain lasting relationship with others is by being deliberate in everything we do with them through building our emotional intelligence. The best relationships are built deliberately, carefully and over time.

Develop your emotional intelligence: Our abilities to build relationships is a manifest of our emotional intelligence. As we mentioned in the first part of this series, our emotional intelligence is all about "*... our capacity to detect, recognise, understand and manage our emotions as well detect, recognise, understand and manage the emotions of others.*" And that, "*There are four elements of emotional intelligence viz: self-awareness, self-management, social-awareness and relationship management.*"

A high emotional intelligence will mean you will understand your own emotional state at any point in time (self-awareness) and also know exactly the right things you need to do to optimise your performance in the circumstances (self-management). It also means you can detect other people's emotional state and know precisely what to do (social awareness and relationship management). Like our intellectual capacities, we can also improve our emotional intelligence. Building your emotional intelligence means you will be able to handle relationship issues wisely. Some of what you must do for that will include:

Be authentic and realistic: Our differences as individual human beings are a great blessing to all of us. Some people are excellent with their hands and others with their minds. Some are skilled at meeting with customers whilst others are more comfortable working in the back offices. We must understand ourselves, what we are good at, what we best enjoy and who we really are. We can always work to improve on our areas of weaknesses but without struggling to be what we are not. Being sincere and authentic is key to our healthy relationships with others. We, each, can see through people who pretend and are duplicitous. And we have only little regard for them.

An integral part of being authentic is being realistic on expectations. That is not in any way suggestive of being unambitious. Rather, it is about stretching but also ensuring that we are practical in achieving our dreams. Being authentic means being truthful and having integrity in everything we say and do.

Listen to others: Transparent and clear communication is fundamental to building healthy relationships. We communicate with others in various ways, such as by email, physical or virtual meetings, phone calls, etc. We also 'communicate' in subtle ways, such as direct eye contact, facial expressions, body movements, etc. But communication is two-way, at least, if two or more people are involved. The sad aspect of it is that most people are good at trying hard to express themselves but are poor at 'actively listening' to others. To work well with other, you have to be an 'active listener'. This means you must understand what the other person is trying to communicate to you. This involves being attentive. It involves asking questions to confirm your understanding, etc. Without effective communication, relationships will ultimately crumble.

Keep your word: A Finnish proverb says, 'The bitter truth is better than a sweet lie.' Adopting to always tell the truth is one of the most successful life policies you can have. It gives you integrity and earns you the trust, respect and confidence of others.

When you promise to make delivery to your customer 'by tomorrow', ensure that the delivery is made either today, preferably, or latest 'by tomorrow', as you promised. Of keeping our words is to deliver on time the reports that our bosses asked for and we committed to; to meet with our subordinates, as promised, to help put them through the spreadsheet they haven't mastered; to buy the sweets that we promised our child in the morning when leaving home for work, etc. If there is any compelling reason as to why you may not fulfil what you promised, ensure that you call ahead the party concerned and discuss. Explain the circumstances and what you are doing to make good your commitment at the earliest and re-negotiated time.

Be punctual: An aspect of 'keeping your word' that needs special mention is punctuality. Every day in our lives we schedule visits, calls, meetings, etc. We do that with our colleagues, clients, professional advisers, etc. Sadly, one of the things that makes things quite difficult for all of us in Nigeria is how we have, perhaps over the last three and a half decades, gotten terrible at being punctual on both 'mundane' and serious appointments. The practice of being late to scheduled meetings and events that we foolishly call 'African time', as if it is something to be proud of, is, rather, something we should all be ashamed of and strive individually and collectively to eliminate in our lives. It is ruining us beyond our comprehension.

Being late in what we promised to do makes us look careless, irresponsible, maybe arrogant. No one likes or trusts 'the careless, the irresponsible and the arrogant'! Thankfully, being punctual is easier than we make it out to be. First, do not choke your day because you want to seem or feel 'busy and important'. Second, be realistic in scheduling your activities.

Give credit: People like to be appreciated for their efforts and results. To strengthen your relationship with others, recognise their efforts and results by appreciating them. Commend them while on your feet or a phone call, a visit or by writing to them. Do all that innocently from your heart and it will show in your eyes, voice and words. Contrary to what many people think, giving people credit for the good they have done doesn't take anything away from you. Only people who are insecure are unable to give credit where it is due. On the other hand, giving credit where it is earned portrays you as an appreciative, sincere and confident leader. It earns you the trust and respect of others and you can expect more good work from them.

Don't gossip! Of the fundamental factors on which we build healthy relationships with others is that we must mean well to them. Meaning well means we are sincere with people. We will tell them the truth as we see it. We advise them whenever it is appropriate, etc. Gossiping about others at our places of work is incongruent with meaning well to the people involved. Unfortunately, gossing about others is prevalent in work environments. So, how do you handle it whenever it comes up?

When others bring up inappropriate issues about others, always divert the discussions away from the topic to something else. If you are unable to do that, simply excuse yourself away if you can. If it is a situation you can neither change the topic nor physically extricate yourself, refuse to be involved in the discussions. With time, you will succeed in creating the reputation of never being part of such little talks and people will begin to avoid it in your presence. On the other hand, if the issues brought up about a non-present third party are indeed of major concern, encourage an appropriate person(s) there to take up the matter with the third-party in a way the third-party could be helped. If you are the appropriate person, then offer to do that! *A life principle to hold is that we should never say behind someone's back what we did not and cannot say to their face.*

Respect boundaries: Of the benefits of building our emotional intelligence is that we can sense and see through what people might be going through. This is not about being sneaky but just alert to changes in human dispositions over the hours and days and weeks in our lives. We should show concern and offer whatever support we can provide whenever we pick up signals. Sometimes it is about saying the right words of encouragements. Other times it could be a visit to the hospital to check on their loved ones. Whatever we may consider appropriate to do, however, must be with due regard and respect to private and/or official boundaries. Do not cross those boundaries unless you are aptly invited to do so.

Mentor your juniors: As individuals, we can be lucky to work for some sixty to seventy years over our lifespans. But even at that, our hyperactive working lifespan is actually no more than some forty years. That means we can easily see three generations taking over national and global economy and politics in our lives. One of the ways to add to your contributions in these natural transitions is to mentor those behind you in your company, industry and local communities. Those of us in our midlives now can easily remember those bosses that held our hands and taught us the tricks of our businesses and life when we were starting out on our careers. We remain endlessly grateful to them. Do the same to the young people in your office and community and in just twenty years you will see them at the top of their careers.

Support the team: Building relationships is about connecting, engaging and adding value to the lives of others. One way to add value to peoples' lives is by supporting them in ways that matters to them. In the workplace, it may be about teaching a subordinate how to improve on their supervisory skills. It could be in helping them on a report they are running late on. It may be about joining the young marketing officer on a call to a prospective client. The more you can help out, the more value you can add to others. This, however, is not about you not doing your work whilst you are busy 'helping' others out. It is also not about doing other people's job.

Rather, it is about doing your job and then supporting others through limited but valuable interventions.

Communicate: We specifically discussed 'listening to others' as being integral to building healthy relationships. However, listening to others is one component of communication in which we serve as 'recipients' of some information. The other component is when we serve as 'senders' of information to others. As senders, we provide all types of information through various media. Sometimes we communicate concepts, stimulatory, empirical, policy or directive information whilst other times it is objective or subjective information we may communicate. Regardless of what type of information and which medium we may use, there are certain standards we must maintain. They include *clarity, completeness* and *conciseness* of the message. Similarly, you should be *empathetic* to the listeners' situation and ensure that you get the *feedback* you require to ascertain their understanding. Over and beyond all that, there must be complete purity in the information you are providing. In other words, whatever information you may provide must stand third party and independent tests of integrity.

Be positive: Daily, each one of us goes through a lot. Good things happen to us as well as what we do not desire. The tendency, therefore, is that we all go through a daily rollercoaster of emotions to varying degrees. To create some level of control through stability, we need to be able to compartmentalise the things that happen to us. One way to do that is to 'resolve' on being positive regardless.

Our positivity does not only help us go through the challenges a lot more easily, but it rubs off on others and also helps them go through personal or common challenges. It is the same reason we also like being close to upbeat and optimistic people even when we may disagree with them in matters of detail. Being positive and upbeat strengthen and motivate us as they do those near us.

Learn to resolve conflicts: Conflicts do occur amongst people in our private and work lives. Conflicts may occur due to several legitimate and wrong reasons. Whatever the reason, the smart entrepreneur and leader must understand the cause, the issues and the personalities involved, as well the environmental and situational contexts that everyone is operating within. Developing your conflict-resolution skills will make it easy for you to help sort out matters before they escalate, hurting relationships and productivity.

With good understanding of situations and people, we can always help resolve potential, emerging and full-blown conflicts. The way to succeed in that is to be understanding of the people and their perspectives; It is to be sincere and well-meaning; It is to be respectful and even discreet if appropriate.

Give out gifts! People like gifts and like those that give them! Interestingly, it is not necessarily about the value of the gift that makes most people happy. Instead, it is the kind thought behind the gift that really matters to most people. Giving out affordable gifts from time to time binds relationships. Inculcate that habit in dealing with your family, friends and business colleagues.

In its simplest, what we should take way with is that building healthy and rewarding relationships is about mutual confidence, trust and respect through sincerity, well-meaning and adding value to the lives of others as well as helping them enhance their productivity. In a workplace, it improves morale, makes teamwork effective and supports personal growth.

25.0 Time Management

"A man who dares to waste one hour of time has not discovered the value of life." – Charles Darwin

After our lives, the core resources that we always 'play' around with to achieve whatever it is we aspire are essentially our *health, intellect* (in this context to include both our minds and our emotions), application of *effort* and *time*. Other key resources are *relationships* and *finances*. But of all the six mentioned, the most important is time.

With the appropriate application of effort and some luck, we can get back or rebuild our health, relationships, knowledge and finances if we damage or lose them. However, time is not recoverable. It is an independent and continuously eroding asset. A second lost is *not* replaceable. We can only make use of the subsequent seconds that nature blesses us with, hopefully better! Ashley Ormon put it succinctly, *"You can't make up for lost time. You can only do better in the future."* Indeed, life itself is nothing but pieces of time we have and what we do within their bounds. Sadly, many of us have no respect for this fundamental dimension of our existence.

Visit any government or private office in Nigeria and chances are that most of the visitors there had no prior appointment. They only showed up hoping to burst into people's offices. They waste their and the officers' time who should, ideally, not entertain them at all. Our weekends are crowded with weddings and parties many of which require that we travel to some distant locations.

But our successes are the positive consequences of the right things *we do* within and not just the *spaces* between the bounds of time we have on Earth. From philosophers to military officers, businessmen and public administrators, it is easy to see that many highly successful people in various fields lived only 'short' lives. Yet, we read about or remember them and feel as if they are still alive. This is because they *did* so much within the time they had on this Earth that we cannot but reckon with them. Simply put, they were highly conscious of time and alert to how best to make use of it.

In the next few pages, we will take up how to make wise use of time. But first, let us start by taking note of a few of the great time wasters we engage in in our environment.

Thoughtless efforts: Obviously, the law of nature is that we must apply effort before we can hope to achieve our desired results. Unfortunately, many of us are yet to distinguish between 'useless effort' and 'productive effort'. A 'useless effort' is the one we apply but which doesn't enhance our chances of achieving worthy output or, even if does, it comes at unjustifiably enormous costs. In other words, a useless effort may be effective but it is inefficient. On the other hand, a productive effort is both effective and efficient with the results achieved justifying the effort applied.

Relationships of no value: As Africans, we are biased by culture to be positively social with other people. That is all fine and good, but we must engage with others sensibly. There are family, friends, colleagues and associates that are highly valuable to us in more ways than we can count. But there are also those who are nothing but time wasters and perhaps negative influences on us. We must minimise our contacts and engagements with the latter category by remembering that we are only as good as the quality of people we keep close to us.

TV, Phones and the social media: We waste so much time watching television and on phone and the social media on the pretext that we get news and for some, entertainment. The truth is that we can get any relevant business, economic and political news on our computers on real time whilst we are doing our productive work. The hours people spend daily watching television and on social media can be put to much more productive use.

Delays and lengthy meetings: As a people, we have come to normalise delays in starting meetings and events as 'African'. That is not only disrespectful to each other, it is sad, shameful, wasteful and highly unproductive. A meeting of nine people whose start is delayed by thirty minutes and in which thirty more avoidable minutes are wasted has cost you, as a participant, one hour of your life. Beyond that, it has cost the local economy a one-man traditional workday.

'Waiting for others': Because of our 'perambulation' approach to achieving certain things, many of us are comfortable waiting for others endlessly. If you visit an office without a prior appointment, you may have to wait endlessly if the 'kind' (read: nonpurposive) official agrees to see you. Sadly because of the same mindset, even officials who have given you an appointment for 11am can keep you waiting endlessly. Absolutely wrong to do and debasing to accept.

As things currently stand, the empirical 'use' of our time suggests that we are, largely, a people contented with putting in effort without much focus on the desired results. This is akin to the running around of a headless a chicken, as they say. Until we discipline ourselves and begin to hold each other responsible to high standards of the good use of our time, we will continue to apply wrong inputs and, unsurprisingly, continue to earn paltry outputs.

> *"An inch of time is an inch of gold*
> *but you can't buy that inch of time with an inch of gold."*
> – Chinese proverb

We have posited that our life is the time we have on this Earth and that the good use of our time is what largely determines our successes. We have brought out some of the individual, social and environmental challenges we have that make us waste so much of our time without notice. We will now take some of the benefits of good time management and also some of the ways to make effective use of our time.

The Benefits of Good Time Management

Doing more: By being alert to the imperative of the good application of our time, we stand a chance of beginning to do so much more in less time and with less effort. By developing our time management skills, we can significantly improve the quality usage of our time and the results we can achieve therefrom.

Lower stress levels: Putting our time to better use has proven ways of lowering our overall stress levels, which in turn enhances our capacity to do more per unit of time.

Creates more opportunities: The more we are able to do in less time, the more opportunities for progress we get in our lives.

Leads to success: Our ability to do more and the greater opportunities that open up in our careers and lives will, naturally, lead to more successes.

How to Develop Time Management Skills

Always start with the mindset: As with most things we discuss, the starting point is always to get our minds to understand, accept and internalise the changes we wish to make. To succeed in life, we have to realise and accept the need to monitor and enforce the optimum use of our time. Without this first step, we will neither be conscious of the time factor itself nor committed to its principled application.

Set your goals correctly: After internalising the philosophical basis of the importance of time management, setting your goals correctly is the starting point of any time management exercise. Without correct goal setting, none of the subsequent actions will lead to desired results.

Prioritise: Once you have your goals set out correctly, the next challenge is to prioritise the activities you will be needing to carry out. Without prioritisation, you may, at best, just end up achieving too little in relation to the resources you commit to endeavours.

Plan your activities: After prioritising your activities, your next task is to plan exactly how to go about doing what you have to do. This will include setting *when* (time), *where* (place) and *how* (method) to do *what* (the activity) you need to do.

Set time limits: A part of planning your activities that deserves special mention is the need to set time limits to your activities. Meetings, visits, etc. should have time windows within which you hope to conclude them. Obviously, you may have to, sometimes spend more time than planned, but with experience, discipline and persistence you will get to be making increasingly better estimates.

Remove non-essential tasks: Sometimes we just feel 'obliged' or perhaps compelled to fill our time with activities irrespective of their importance and ultimate value add. This is completely unnecessary. Eliminating non-essential tasks will free your body and mind to do the more important things that add true value to your life. Don't feel guilty having free time.

Create a routine: Developing and building a routine is a sure way of enhancing our efficiency. Wake up each morning around the same time. Create specific times for reviewing and working on documents as well as office meetings, checking work e-mails and responding to them, etc. Obviously, we have to alter our routines from time to time to meet emerging realities. But having a working template will generally help us well. One of the major benefits of having a routine is that even other people you deal with will get to know your routine and respect it, thereby helping you further.

Slow down! Quite counter-intuitively, one of the ways to improve the good usage of your time is by slowing down. By slowing down, we are able to see things more clearly and experience them in greater details. The clarity and experience both enhance the quality of our lives and our capacity to do better, more and with less effort.

Specifically in Nigeria, I like to always suggest some actions to help free our time. As Carl Sandburg put it, *"Time is the coin of your life. It is the only coin you have and you can determine how it will be spent. Be careful lest you let other people spend it for you."*

- Always make appointments to visit people and for people to visit you. If you will, for genuine reasons be late to appointments, call well ahead and inform the other party. Be realistic by telling them when you expect to be with them. Please, don't say you will be there 'in five minutes' when you sincerely know it will take you thirty! Tell them it will take you thirty. No one will kill you!

- Keep reasonable, practical gaps between appointments, so that meeting extensions and traffic situations can be accommodated without being late to subsequent appointments.

- Avoid looking irresponsible, incompetent and having to apologise for being late to appointments by setting out early.

- Respect other people's time and ask that yours be respected also. Extract yourself from the terrible attitude we shamelessly call 'African time' and demand that others don't mess with your time either.

- You don't have to attend all weddings and parties for goodness' sake! Set criteria about those that you should attend and stick to it.

- Focus on those activities that are of importance and avoid those that just keep you busy without many positive returns.

26.0 Self-Management

We have, in a rather piecemeal style and from technical perspectives, taken up a few personal but important issues that can help or hinder our chances of achieving successes in our careers and lives. Some of the topics covered included time management, relationship management, getting things done, prioritisation, etc. Now we will take up self-management that will put all of those and some more critical success factors together.

Self-management refers to an individual's ability to manage their feelings, thoughts and behaviours in a way that they are able to optimise their overall productivity. It is the result of self-awareness that makes it possible for an individual to understand their personal responsibility in the various spheres and situations of their lives and be able to do what they need to do to discharge their obligations honourably and creditably. An individual with strong self-management skills can always do what they appropriately need to do in any situation or circumstance. Such an individual would, for instance, be capable of controlling their anger and know how best to respond when treated unfairly by their boss in the workplace. They can maintain focus and achieve the required productivity while working from home by eliminating and avoiding likely home-setting distractions.

The benefits of great self-management skills are myriad. In research reported by the California Office to Reform Education, 'CORE', it was found out that self-control in children as young as age 5 can reasonably "… *predict important life outcomes such as high school completion, physical health, income, single parenthood, substance dependence and criminal involvement.*" Specifically, children with better self-management abilities at the age of 4 were 40% more likely to complete university education by age 25. Similarly, Walter Mischel's (disputed by some) 'Marshmallow Test' showed that the ability to 'delay gratification' at age 4 predicts academic and social competence and the capacity to cope with stresses later in life.

In adulthood, self-management skills enhance our efficiency, thereby improving our personal and workplace performances. Self-management improves our mental and physical health as well as overall wellbeing. Our self-management skills make us reliable and predictable with other people. These two qualities ease many things for us and those associated with us. But, I think, one of the best benefits of self-management skills is in improving our private and official relationships with family, friends, colleagues, business associates, etc.

The following are the four elements of self-management:

Self-awareness: The bedrock of self-management is self-awareness. Every day, our minds process billions of inputs and we make decisions out of them consciously and subconsciously. To be adept at doing the right things in the various situations we find ourselves in daily, we must be alert to these multitude of inner activities that influence our feelings, thoughts and desires. Understanding and monitoring the linkages of these three to the likely actions we may take is crucial to our successes. Being perceptive to what is happening within us and wisely choosing from our optional responses is key to success.

Self-regulation: We all experience varying emotions daily. This is all well and normal. However, certain people can experience volatile emotions, making them feel much higher highs and lower lows. These bizarre high 'peaks' and grotesque low 'valleys' can cause out of control swings and spins in the behaviours of individuals. We sometimes see these people reacting violently to seemingly innocent errors by others that should have caused no more than an irritation.

But self -regulation is not about supressing our natural emotional states. Rather, it is about being alert to and managing them through deliberate, effective and astute control. Self-regulation is also about developing coping strategies that make it possible to positively handle difficult emotions. The ability to self-regulate is the result of a person's awareness of their internal rumblings as well as an external capacity to handle them.

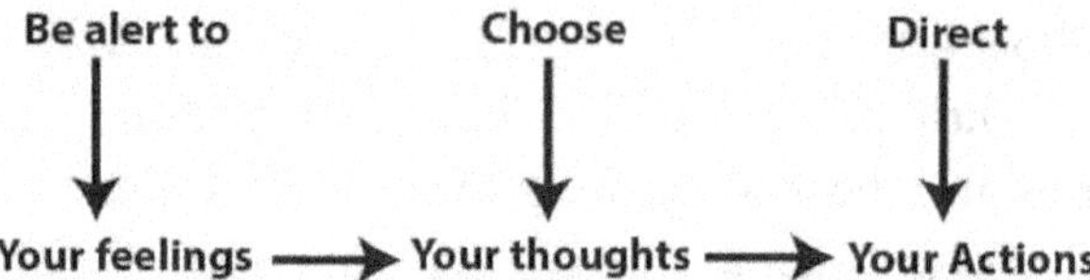

Figure 26.1: Link between feelings, thoughts and actions
(© Musbahu El Yakub)

Self-accountability: Understanding and accepting that we are responsible for what we do is a pillar on which our self-management skills are developed. Self-accountability is about taking ownership of both our thought processes as well as the actions we take externally. By accepting this responsibility, we empower ourselves to be able to do what needs to be done irrespective of what may be happening within and around us.

Self-motivation: This refers to the capability to do what is right no matter the inconveniences, difficulties and challenges in a situation. A self-motivated individual can anticipate, plan and act on both ongoing and future-expected endeavours. The self-motivated individual is driven by internal desire to do the right things and achieve success. Two integral components of self-motivation are *initiative* and *diligence*. Initiative is about an individual's wherewithal and willingness to start what needs to be started. Initiative demonstrates a person's ability to develop ideas on issues as well as take action to convert the ideas into tangible, desired results. Initiative involves creativity, innovation and risk-management. On the other hand, diligence is neatly defined by the etymology dictionary as *'constant and earnest effort to accomplish what is undertaken'*, and that it is the *'conscientiousness in paying proper attention to a task; giving the degree of care required in a given situation'*.

How to Develop Self-Management Skills

If there is just one skill set that we need to succeed in life, those shall be self-management skills. These are the skills that we require to get the right things done correctly and efficiently in any and every situation we may find ourselves. For instance, a well self-managed entrepreneur striving to build a business would have no problem waking up early on a cold morning, after a late night at work, to get ready to go to work again even as they would have preferred to remain in bed for three more hours. Pulling out of bed may not be easy in the circumstance, but the self-managed budding entrepreneur is clear that it is compelling to go to work and get the work done if they are to stand any chance to succeed. That decision and its execution will be based on the understanding and acceptance of the imperative to do the right thing and not just what is situationally convenient.

Self-management skills are built on certain simple but core principles of success that are unchanging in time and space. In my opinion, there is just a tripod of these principles:

You must work hard to succeed: Working hard is the executory part of getting anything right and good in life done. But do not get caught in the 'work smart not hard' arguments. 'Hard work' actually comprises both a *smart mental* as well as a *physical exertion* components. Consequently, 'smart' work is an integral component of 'hard' work with an emphasis on the intellectual rather than the physical dimensions of work. But both are required as complements to each other. The complementarity of the two is succinctly brough out by Tim Notke when he said, *"Hard work beats talent when talent doesn't work hard"*.

You must be honest: Our technical skills and the relationships we have can always help open doors for us. But in the long run, nothing gives us honour and sustains the opportunities we get as well as create new ones than being honest. People might sometimes find your truths inconvenient, but you will always be respected for it. The English proverb that 'honesty is the best policy' is timeless and fundamental to success. In every situation you ever find yourself, you should never have to think about telling the truth. It should be a permanent and default setting of your mind.

You must continuously develop yourself: In spite of the technologies around that do make things so much easier for us, our lives will continue to get more challenged, perhaps because of globalisation, opportunities, cultural mixes, etc. The only way we can always understand our place and role in the scheme of events and be able to do what we should rightly do is try to continuously understand people, events and things. Developing yourself will help you be able to put issues in their appropriate place regardless of the all the noise and distractions around.

Life throws stuff at us, good and bad. Often, we also attract stuff at us, good and bad also. We should be very alert and good at trying to do the conscionable things and making corrections when we err. According to George Bernard Shaw, *"Life isn't about finding yourself. Life is about creating yourself"*. What he meant is that we should continuously strive to develop ourselves towards being the best we can.

How do we develop the alert mind, the right mindset and an active body that is always ready to get the appropriate things done?

Start with taking care of yourself: The cabin crew in an aeroplane would always announce that in the event of an emergency, you should first put on your oxygen mask before you help those in need around you. The logic is simple: If you do not protect yourself first in that situation, you may pass out before you even complete helping the needy person near you. It is the same thing in most other things in life. But taking care of yourself is not about wanton greed. Rather, it is about developing yourself. It is about preparing and strengthening yourself in the areas you need to help yourself, your loved ones, your business and indeed the world. Simply put, do the right things to take legitimate care of yourself and only then will you be able to do so much more for others.

Always make thoughtful decisions: The first evidence you would notice as you begin to develop your self-management skills is that you will be making decisions better and faster even when they are a little difficult. But there two lanes on the decision-making highway: There is a fast lane for issues against which you have already internalised principles of action on them. If, for instance, a customer unknowingly pays you more cash than they were invoiced, you would, without any delay, alert the customer and return the over-payment. This doesn't require 'any thought' and no time is wasted. On the other hand, if you are considering going into a business that you have never been involved with in the past, you will need to study it a lot. You will need to meet with several experts and people experienced in the business before you will be able to finally make a decision one way or the other. In this situation, you should take your time and not rush into making decisions.

Be purposeful: The foundation for doing the right things in life starts with the understanding of our purpose. Unless we know what we are here for or what good we wish to achieve, we will 'wobble and fumble', gathering no moss like the proverbial rolling stone! Being purposeful is fundamental to the design of the life we want to live. It gives us the long-term picture of what we are or are striving to be. Sometimes we create our own purpose, like a person who runs a foundation to help provide start-up capital for budding entrepreneurs in order to help to create wealth, employment and overall public good. Other times, political, social or economic circumstances can force a purpose upon us, like an engineer that leaves their highly paid employment to go into politics because they are unhappy with local political developments and want to help alter the fate of their people. Purpose makes us live honourable, responsible and focussed lives.

Be conscientious: Once we are clear about our purpose in life, the next challenge will be about being alert to doing everything that will support the continuous achievement of that purpose. Similarly, we have to be alive to all those things that will undermine our effort towards living the purposeful live we aspire to. Being conscientious is the 'short-term' leg of being purposeful in the long run. It makes us deliberate on the seemingly little things of life, but which may have terrible short- and long-term consequences. Being conscientious makes us conscious of the time that we have on this Earth and commits us to make the best use of it.

Be diligent: It is easy to want to live a purposeful life and even try to be conscientious. However, we may still fail in achieving our purpose because we aren't diligent in what we do. Being diligent is about being thorough and complete in whatever it is that needs to be done. Mentally, it is about a presence of mind in everything we do and physically it is about the capacity to actually get things done. Diligence is an integral part of self-management because it is required to be able to beneficially seize opportunities as well as solve problems as they may arise.

Develop your compartmentalisation skills: Compartmentalisation is just that 'dispassionate' ability and willingness to assess and value everything around us appropriately and respond by putting them exactly where they belong. Compartmentalisation is that 'out-of-nowhere' capacity to get things right. It refers to the ability and willingness to analyse everything happening around us and attaching an appropriate value. Based on the value attached, an intelligent action is then taken.

Compartmentalisation is what makes it possible for self-managed people to take a difficult but right road when the convenient but wrong road is crowded by everyone else. A highly compartmentalised person will process, internalise and 'box' up a massive loss they just suffered and, nonetheless, do the right thing on other issues in the next minutes. Compartmentalisation makes us highly adaptive to the vagaries of life even as we fight honourably and relentlessly. It is what breaks the marathon that life is into piecemeal segments that we handle wisely and sort of effortlessly. It is of the greatest quality of self-managed individuals.

Learn from the past and others: Of compartmentalisation ability that should be brought out on its own is the willingness to learn from the past but without getting stuck in it. We should be able to retain what works in the past and can work now but should be comfortable to make positive changes where required or if necessary. Similarly, we should learn from others and be able to build better. The world gets better in science and technology only because the present crop of scientists and engineers are standing tall on the shoulders of giants of the past. It is no gainsaying that what we could never achieve what we are able to do today without having the past knowledge passed on to us by those people that lived thousands of years ago.

Be a positive experience for others: Just recently, I was in a Nigerian central state for some work. At the onset, I knew that I would need some assistants for the period that work would last. When I told a friend resident in the state what I needed, he suggested three young persons known to him. On my team's arrival in the state, we met with the recommended individuals. Their qualifications met our requirements and in return I told them what the standards we expected were. We agreed all details and the young persons worked with us for the duration the work lasted.

We worked well with those young people and each of us had, undoubtedly, a teaching-learning and pleasant experience. We are still in touch even after the project is fully completed, commissioned, and handed over.

It is the reality of life that we meet scores of people every day. Some we only spend a few seconds with whilst others we spend hours on end with them. Some of those people we probably meet every day whilst others we may never get to meet again. Whatever is the extent and frequency of contact, it is appropriate that we have the intention and do work to give them a positive experience of being with us. That will make us conscious of whatever we do with them and its likely long-term impact on each of us.

27.0 Keep Your Word

"Your word is your honour. If you say you're going to do something, then you need to do it." – Joyce Meyer

Every day of our lives, we make commitments to people and they also make to us as well. The people might be socially junior, senior or at the same level with us. The commitments might range from the personal to the official and from the 'mundane' to the serious. It is a multi-dimensional matrix of possibilities that we must contend with. Regardless of the mix, however, one thing should remain constant: we must keep our word when we give it and we have the right to demand the same standard from others when they give theirs' to us.

Without any shred of doubt, one of the fundamental causes of problems in our country is that many people of all ages, social and financial status have, unfortunately, lost the sense of honour in keeping their word. Businesspersons have no remorse failing to deliver goods and services as they promised their clients and customers. Politicians and civil servants have no shame in breaking promises they made to the electorate or the public contract they agreed to.

As an entrepreneur, you will often make commitments to your business associates just as your business associates will frequently make commitments to you. Your raw materials supplier could promise to deliver certain additives to you by a particular date. Your customer might commit to settle a bill on or before the due date on the invoice, etc. Failure of the raw material supplier to deliver by the promised date or that of the customer to make the payment as committed can disrupt your production run and hamper your ability to deliver goods to your customers or in the latter case undermine your capacity to settle your own debt with your creditors, thereby negatively impacting on your reputation. Similarly, your failure to pay your supplier as agreed will amount to a default in contract and a breach of trust. Both can make your supplier impose more stringent payments terms on you.

When we make promises verbally or otherwise, we are actually entering into 'contract' even if there is no intent for legal relations. The failure to keep our word has negative consequences some of which may be mild, not-so-obvious and into the future whilst others may be dire, obvious and immediate. Some of the negative consequences are:

It damages our relationships: When we fail to keep our word with others, we strain and damage our relationships with them. In addition, it creates conflicts with and lowers our own self-esteem both of which make things difficult that are otherwise easy.

Failing to keep our word is a strong indicator of our values and standards as individuals and organisations. It negatively affects us and our businesses in far-reaching ways than we can imagine. It is a demonstration of our disrespect of others and ourselves. In return, others will also have no respect for us and will deliberately, and rightly too, make everything we try to do with them more laborious.

It kills opportunities for us: Once we fail to keep our word on an issue, people have the right not to believe any other thing from us. This failure that we may, wrongly, take for granted will kill future opportunities for us as the people are not, rightly, disposed to trust whatever it is we may tell them again.

If we promise we are going to do something but fail to do it, our word will eventually hold an utterly negative symbolism of our integrity, thereby losing the trust of others. People will not take our word for what we want them to be. Keeping our word is always easier than facing the fallouts of the failure. We lose opportunities and will need to work several times harder to re-earn the trust we lost.

On the other hand, when we always keep our word, the benefits are momentous. They include:

It opens up opportunities for us: When people trust us, they give us more opportunities. Cosmas Maduka, the Chairman/President of Coscharis Group often discussed how, at critical points in his business career, he enjoyed trade credit support from his Japanese suppliers because he always kept his word. Every person that keeps their word will have limitless opportunities thrown at them.

We get to deepen our relationships: When we always keep our word, the relationships we build with others get deepened. People trust us without conditions and do not doubt what we say. Similarly, they get comfortable with us and don't question or second-guess us in our interactions with them.

We learn to be alert: To be good at keeping our word, we must be thoughtful and contemplative of everything we are about to say. This means we weigh and consider every thought in our mind before we utter them out as promises to others. We, therefore, don't take lightly what we say to others or otherwise commit to them.

We develop self-trust and build confidence in ourselves: When we develop the capacity always to keep our word, we develop self-trust and confidence in ourselves. We also eliminate feelings of guilt and regrets that always come with the failing to keep our word as well as the shame that comes with it. Similarly, our resolve to keep our word, even when things sometimes go off our plan, helps to develop a strong character in us that does nothing but help to bring good to us.

It is the right thing to do: Failing to keep our word is wrong as it disappoints, often hurts, others in ways that we do not wish to be disappointed or hurt. Failure to keep our word can cost others their time, money, opportunities and even life. Keeping our word is simply the right thing to do.

Why People Fail to keep Their Word

Our objective here is to ultimately learn how we can achieve and maintain a one hundred per cent fulfilment rate of our promises. We want to get to the point where everyone in our lives, from family, friends to business associates and acquittances, have complete and unreserved faith in our words. Let us try to understand why many people don't always keep their word. Some of the reasons are:

We never had the intention to keep our word! *Ab initio*, we may not have had the sincere intention to fulfil what we said we were going to do. Once we do not have that initial intention, we can hardly get to discharge our pledges at the right time, the right way and the right place as we promised. Even if we do, it would likely be only half-hearted and incomplete.

We do not want to renegotiate: Sometimes, we are just averse to requesting for a renegotiation of the terms we sincerely agreed to at first but which, for possibly legitimate reasons, need to be reconsidered by all parties. We may 'feel bad' having to call for a renegotiation even when that is the right and sensible thing to do in the circumstance. Unfortunately, reluctance to renegotiate may lead to complete failure to fulfil the promise.

We are not alert: Often, we just are not alert to the implications of what we say to others. In such situations, we may make statements without appreciating the fact that they are commitments to which we should be bound.

On our way out to work, our child could ask us, "Dad/mum, would you buy me a bicycle?" Not a few parents would be tempted to respond affirmatively, just to 'dismiss' the child but not actually meaning to buy the bicycle. However, our affirmation is a pledge to buy a bicycle and our failure to deliver on that has several untoward consequences. First, the child cannot process that we didn't do what we promised. Second, the child will not take our word seriously at other times when we may 'mean to be earnest'. Thirdly and grievously, we are unwittingly teaching the child not to take their own word purposefully either.

We forget what we have committed to: Other times, we forget what we committed to. This is not necessarily because we did not have the intention to do what we promised but because we have failed to be sufficiently organised to remember what we covenanted. We may, for instance, have been sincere about buying the bicycle for the child, but we just failed to register it mentally in our minds amongst the activities of the day, thereby letting it slip through the cracks. Unfortunately, our sincere intentions are not always sufficient. In addition, we must be committed, organised and executory about what we averred to.

We over-commit: In this situation, we are simply unrealistic about the limited time we have to do all the things we committed to over a specific period of time. Like the previous cause of failure, this is usually not because we were not sincere but because we may not be sufficiently realistic and organised about how much time and effort we need to get the things on our plate done.

It is 'nothing': In our national environment, we have, sadly, come to take certain commitments we make as being 'nothing'. We take such pledges for granted and have neither problem nor remorse in breaking them. It doesn't even occur to us! This should be repulsive, as there is absolutely nothing like 'nothing' in a promise. As it is said, a promise is a debt unpaid.

If we promise to revert back to our customer 'before the close of business' on an issue, it is not good enough to revert back to them the following morning! We promised to revert back 'before close business', the good and honourable thing is to revert back 'before the close of business' that day. Simple.

We promised what we know was 'impossible': When we suggest or accept to do what we know is not realistic or possible, we are setting ourselves to fail. For instance, an entrepreneur running an import clearing agency might pledge to clear some consignment from the port and deliver same to a client within a week. But from experience, the entrepreneur probably knows that given the procedural requirements, the clearing of the consignment within a week is close to an impossibility. Such a promise is unlikely to be kept.

We didn't believe: In this case, we promise what we don't believe. Now even if what we promised is achievable, our unbelief will make it difficult for us to deliver on it. A subtle but highly dominating feature of the human mind is its capacity to make the body successfully 'work' towards what it believes no matter how difficult or inconvenient. The corollary of the that is also the capacity of the mind to undermine what the body does if it (the mind) doesn't believe in it. The moment we don't believe in what we are promising, we are unlikely to carry it out fully and satisfactorily.

We think that we can compartmentalise: Sometimes we think we can compartmentalise by keeping our promises in one situation but be nonchalant about it in others. For instance, we may think that we can always keep our promise to our spouse but can get away with a standard lower than that at work. However, the tendency of human behaviour is always to be reinforced in a particular direction. This means failing to keep our promise at our place of work will ultimately always hurt our selective desire to fulfil our promise to our spouse.

How to Develop the Capacity to Keep Your Word

We can now take up some of the ways we can develop, strengthen and protect our capacity always to keep our word. There are two elements to that: Those that have to do with the mind and those to do with the body. Those to do with the mind are:

Understand and desire the benefits of keeping your word: The first step in beginning to fully and always keep our word is to understand and desire all the good that comes with it. As discussed previously, keeping our word is the right and honourable thing to consistently do. The benefits of having other people to unconditionally and always have faith in what we say have no quantifiable measure.

Internalise the right philosophy: After understanding and accepting the immeasurable benefits of keeping our word, the next step is to internalise the foundational philosophy necessary for doing that. This means we become resolved, at all times, to discharge whatever and everything we agreed to. This implies that each time we make a promise, we unreservedly have a sincere and complete intention and commitment to fulfil it.

Adopt the right principles: To be steadfast in keeping the promises we make, there are a few things that we have to be clear about, which are a fall out of the reasons why we don't always keep our word. For instance, we have to believe in each promise that we make. So, before the clearing agent in the last example commits to clear and deliver a consignment within one week to their client, the agent must sincerely believe that the job can be done as promised. Similarly, we should accept that sometimes we may have legitimate reasons to call for a renegotiation of the terms we initially agreed to. The only conditions to this are that we should give as much notice as is possible and we must respect the rights of the other party and be honourable in the renegotiation process.

Presence of mind: Often, we make statements without realising that we are actually making a pledge. In the example we gave last, the affirmation a parent gives the child that asked for a bicycle is a promise to buy a bicycle. To achieve a one hundred per cent fulfilment rate of our promises, therefore, we must be conscious of the implications of the words we utter and the written details above the dotted lines we signed on. Simply put, presence of mind, in our context here, is about being mentally alert to the things we say and promise to do to others.

Set your standard: There are times when it is pragmatic and optimum to flow with the crowd. But there are times we must be willing to stand out and away from the crowd. Always keeping to our pledges is one area we must be ready to stand out. In addition, as you strive to do as you gave your word, demand the same standard from the people you deal with.

Be consistent: There are areas in which it is desirable to compartmentalise our thinking and actions. However, in anything and everything to do with keeping our word, we must strive to be consistent no matter who or what is involved. That means we should make it to the wedding ceremony we committed to attend as punctually as we would attend a multi-million Naira business meeting with a client. That is to say we must take seriously each promise we make. Consistency disciplines the body and eases the mind while dissonance weakens the body and confuses the mind.

The elements to do with the body include:

Be organised: One of the chief causes of failing to keep our word is because we either think we can do what may not be realistic or we just want to appear to be busy either to ourselves or to others. This is both counterproductive and hurtful. While it may also be because we want to capture opportunities, it would, in reality, over time, only cast us as persons who fail in keeping their promise. The antidote to this failure is to be organised. This means we should be realistic about how much we can do over a time interval. Scheduling our 'to do' list is a crucial task that we should take seriously.

Give your word less often: Yes, we frequently have to give our word if we are to be able to seize opportunities. However, how often we give our word must match our capacity to discharge same while also retaining our sanity. Given our individual capacities, time available and the resources we need to deploy, over-committing should always be avoided. Being able to say 'No' and negotiating for what is convenient and realistic are very crucial if we are to be able to always do what we say 'Yes' to.

Take small steps: Our ability to keep our word always should be developed the same way an athlete physically and mentally improves their mental discipline and motor controls. It is initially incremental and cautious and then ambitious later. This means we begin by giving less of our word but ensuring that we keep each. Gradually and with continuous discharge of the 'small' number of promises we make, we begin to take on and do more. While building this skill, the interesting and encouraging thing you will realise is that people will be a lot more understanding with your 'No' than you would have thought.

Keeping our word is a demonstration of a congruence between our inner thoughts and outer actions. It is evidence of our integrity and good character. It is a long-term determinant of our honour, peace of mind and success.

28.0 Providing Leadership

Every endeavour that involves two or more people will require leadership to be provided if it is to be successful. Families, communities, businesses and governments require leadership if they are to flourish. Leadership, which has always been needed and will always be needed, shall be our subject now.

Management and Leadership: One of the first confusions that people have is in trying to understand the difference(s) between *management* and *leadership*. First to be aware of is that there is a wide overlap between the roles and responsibilities of managers and leaders. However, there are also differences of *purpose, approach* and *emphasis*. Let us try to understand by contrasting them.

Up to the beginning of the industrial age, collective human activities were initiated and 'managed' by individuals who were essentially leaders (even if their specific roles and approaches varied due to differences in their responsibilities). From heads of business associations to spiritual leaders, military leaders and Kings, leadership was bestowed on the strength of the competence and character and, sometimes, birthrights of individuals. With the advent of the industrial age, the need for 'professionals' that can enhance efficiency and productivity by managing resources and processes became imperative. This led to the demand for trained managers or the 'organisation man'. However, the obsession with the training of more managers over the last sixty years, I would say, has contributed, rather unwittingly, to the loss of focus on developing true leadership skills. Thankfully, there is an emerging renaissance on leadership training as a result of globalisation, information overload and ethical and environmental considerations.

Essentially, a manager is a person with technical skills, knowledge and/or expertise that coordinates activities to achieve immediate and short-term goals by working with others that they closely supervise directly or indirectly. Management, the role of the manager, is about managing resources through planning and carrying out tasks for the purposes of achieving set goals. The functions of management are typically conducted in formal organisations, even as they are beneficial to informal settings, too. According to one school of thought, the functions of management are planning, organising, staffing, directing and controlling. Managers might be generalists but are usually experts with good knowledge and skills that enable them to guide their workers daily.

Leadership, on the other hand, is about the capacity of an individual, the leader, to influence and inspire others towards achieving major objectives. It is fundamentally about visioning and setting direction/strategy that managers and other followers will willingly carry out. Leadership is also about getting others to be passionate about long-term objectives and committed to the day-to-day grind of working towards those objectives whilst the leader gives them reasonable operational space. Leaders must have the foresight, knowledge and charisma to get people motivated towards objectives that may seem far into the horizon. Successful leaders are emotionally intelligent people that understand their followers well, set high ethical and moral standards for them and generally shape group cultures.

Beyond being emotionally brilliant, a good leader becomes great if they also have the technical skills of a good manager. Conversely, beyond being technically competent, a good manager becomes great if they also have the emotional intelligence of a good leader.

The Benefits of Leadership: Leadership is required in all social spheres and at all levels of formal and informal organisations. Some benefits of leadership include:

- Leadership helps to set a vision for a formal organisation or an informal group. Without visionary leadership, people will lack the focus required to achieve any objective.

- Beyond setting a vision, leadership sets the strategy and direction to be taken to achieve objectives. Without strategy and direction, goals, no matter how lofty they might be, will remain nothing but pipe dreams.
- Leadership sets and shapes the culture of organisations.
- Leaders are generally great teachers and mentors, making it possible for organisations to sustain dreams and aspirations for centuries on end.

Traits of Leaders: From our childhood escapades to university and through working careers and life in entrepreneurship, we have all come across all sorts of leaders that could inspire others to get things done. As children and senior adults, we have also read about great leaders in business, politics, government, civil resistance, etc. Names like Martin Luther King, Jr., Sakichi Toyoda, Nelson Mandela, etc. easily come to mind. What are some of the common traits of these greats?

- Great leaders tend always to be emotionally intelligent. They understand themselves and others well.
- They are able to think ahead and 'see' certain things that most others don't.
- They are great communicators and are able to get people interested and committed to aspirations regardless of difficulties.
- They are self-motivated and are able to remain upbeat, positive and confident even in trying times.
- They are interested in other people and alert to tell-tale signs of loss of enthusiasm and can remotivate people.
- They are always able to focus on the big picture.
- Great leaders hold themselves responsible of their and their followers' actions and don't make excuses.

- They set core objectives and fundamental strategies, allowing 'managers' and followers room to deal with tactical details within agreed operating principles.
- They are able to work with all shades of people and handle each well.
- Great leaders are passionate, persistent and resilient. They see as temporary setbacks and minor irritations what others consider as failures.

If you ask me, the four most important factors that help retain the loyalty of followers to great leaders are the leaders' integrity, competence, resilience and the ability to understand and keep their followers interested and committed.

So far, we have discussed some of the differences between management and leadership, the benefits of leadership and the traits of leaders. We shall now take up how you can develop yourself into a great leader.

How to Develop into a Great Leader

Most good entrepreneurs tend to be good managers, too. But to be a great entrepreneur, you will need to be a great leader as well. Being a great leader and a great entrepreneur is not only about the turnover and profitability of your business. Rather, it is also about how you and your business affect others positively. Each of your stakeholders should be impacted positively by you and your business. Again, it is not always about the magnitude of your impact but its sincerity, originality and quality. So, what are some of the ways you could develop yourself into a great leader capable of providing leadership to your people and enterprise?

As always, start from your mind: So far, you have probably lost count of how many times I have mentioned that everything starts from the mind. Yes, everything we wish to do and do well must start from our minds. Unless we clearly process and internalise it, we are not likely to commit and put in the effort required to succeed at it. Starting with our minds here means we consciously make a resolution to be great leaders. That includes understanding what leadership is and how great leaders develop and conduct themselves.

Read about great leaders: After your resolution to become a great leader, a good starting point for leadership development is reading the autobiographies of great leaders. Read about great emperors of the past, the military generals, the sports coaches, the great political leaders and entrepreneurs that succeeded against unbelievable odds, etc. There are great leaders in every endeavour and you can a lot learn from each of them.

Develop your technical skills: We have already mentioned that managers must be knowledgeable and skilled in their trades or professions. But technical skills are also required by great leaders. Technical knowledge and skills make it possible for a leader to understand what is being discussed or proposed. But beyond just understanding the issues at hand, technical skills make it possible for the leader to add value through provision of wise and better ways to get objectives achieved.

Learn to listen to yourself: Every day, our minds process billions of inputs. We draw conclusions and make decisions, often subconsciously. Listening to ourselves means picking the right thoughts and dropping the wrong ones in our internal discourse. We cannot lead others well if we cannot lead ourselves first and well. To lead ourselves well, it is crucial that that we are able to listen to ourselves and act deliberately.

Lead yourself: At a low level, the benefit of being able to listen to ourselves is that we can understand what is going on right inside us. At the high level, listening to ourselves is the starting point of providing self-leadership. Unless you are unable to conduct yourself appropriately through self-leadership, you can easily lose the moral rights to lead others. You may still have the legal authority, but you are unlikely to get the most out of others.

You must be in pursuit of a vision: You cannot be a leader without a vision that you are excited and captivated by. You have to also be able to convince others to buy into your vision. Having a clear vision is, perhaps, the first condition you should meet for others to accept to follow you. A vision is about your ultimate, larger-than-life strategic objective. It must be grand, exciting, captivating and alluring to you and your followers.

Listen to and understand others: One of the areas in which great leaders are always ahead of others is in their ability to listen to and understand others. The followers of a great leader may not even need to speak for the leader to have a good sense of what they may be thinking or going through. Listening to others requires discipline, patience and emotional intelligence. Listening to others means we can deeply understand them beyond what they say and what they do. It is a key requirement for us to be able to lead them effectively.

Engage with others: Great leaders are excellent in engaging with others at the highest levels. Their engagements with others is always two-way and about the issues that they are both passionate about. As a leader, your engagements should inspire, motivate, educate and reward others. You have to come up with new ideas and projects. You must trust and empower their followers, etc. Even when you empower others, though, you are to take responsibility when things go wrong.

Be sincere: Leadership requires that you have not only a legal authority on the people that follow you but also a moral right. You can only earn the moral right to lead others by doing the right things you need to do and also conducting yourself impeccably in easy and tough times. Set high standards and be a congruent leader whose followers do not second-guess their motivation.

Unfortunately, many people in leadership positions in our environment do not take the issue of morality seriously. They assume that their legal authority is sufficient for them to exercise control and influence over their followership. This is, however, only true to a limited extent and will always be costly in the long run.

Other issues: As a leader, it is vital that you continuously grow your network with the right people. Learn and make your organisation learn from mistakes made. You should ceaselessly develop yourself and your people. It is imperative to work hard with resolve, be a role model and show the right examples to your people. You must be humble, proactive and responsive without shying away from problems. You must always be there for your people. Quite honestly, leadership is so much more about discharging responsibilities than enjoying privileges. Finally, you have to take your health seriously through taking good foods, exercises and as may be recommended by your doctor.

Figure 28.1: Providing leadership
(Image credit: Photo by Jehyun Sung on Unsplash)

Chapter 5

"Plan ahead or find trouble at your footsteps." - Confucius

29.0 Handling Business Crisis

Whenever we come up with business ideas, test their feasibility and draw up plans, what preoccupies our minds are the actions we will carry out over time and the success that awaits us. But the reality is that many entrepreneurs and their business hit head winds and run into difficulties. Difficulties and even crises do happen in business. What can you do about them?

Understanding what, typically, causes disasters and what philosophies and practices should be adopted will minimize the likelihood of their occurrence or the severity of the damage they could cause. Let's take a single case for review.

In 1982, the curious deaths of seven people in the United States were traced to the ingestion of Tylenol, which was criminally tampered and laced with potassium cyanide. How did the manufacturers of Tylenol, Johnson and Johnson, handle the massive negative publicity and consequential impact on their business value?

In 1981, prior to the unfortunate deaths, seventeen per cent of Johnson and Johnson net profit was contributed by the Tylenol brand. By the time the incidence happened, marketers predicted that the company would never recover from the sabotage. However, only two months later, Tylenol, earlier withdrawn by the company in the wake of the crisis, was back in the market with tamper-proof package and amidst massive media campaign.

Johnson and Johnson earned public sympathy in the way they handled the Tylenol case. What did they do differently from such other international crises as Chernobyl and Bhopal that were considered poorly handled?

Johnson and Johnson placed the safety and interest of the customers and public first! The company withdrew thirty-one million bottles of Tylenol capsules from store shelves. Replacement products in safer tablet form were also offered free of charge.

James Burke, then Chairman of Johnson and Johnson, provided great leadership not just in the promptness of the recall and replacement, but in the transparency and forthrightness in dealing with the media and public enquiries. Within a month, the Chairman was at a press conference able to give a full, transparent and detailed chronology of the what the company had done. It was clear that the Chairman and the company were in control of the situation.

Consequently, a year later, the company's share of the analgesics market, which had tumbled from 37% to 7% had recovered up to 30%. That was phenomenal. The growth of the company had continued in various product lines since then. In addition, Tylenol was re-launched with a tamper-proof packaging seal and introduced caplets. This solution is seen less as an innovation or a great crisis plan but more as a crisis solution that focused on public safety and consumer peace of mind. This philosophy itself was a reflection of an already existing value proposition culture of the company.

Crises can be as a result of sabotage, as in the case of Johnson and Johnson. It could be as a result of too much debt, a global financial meltdown, as in 2007, or a pandemic, as in Covid-19. It could be because of a fire incidence or flood. Quite honestly, it could be because of anything under the Sun. Whatever it is that triggers a crisis, you should have honourable and pragmatic principles of its management backed by transparent actions.

What is crisis management? Crisis management in business is the identification of a threat to a business, the development of appropriate responses and carrying out requisite actions with a view to minimising the damage of the threat. Crisis management is about dealing with sudden and significant negative events that could threaten the functions of a business or even its survival.

The goal of crisis management is to minimise the damage that could otherwise the impact on a business. Beyond minimising damages to business, wise crisis management can actually serve as springboards to unanticipated opportunities and benefits!

First, accept that something has gone wrong: Without accepting that something has gone wrong, you and your team are likely to be in denial and your actions will be discordant and self-destroying. Accepting that things have gone wrong will enable you to estimate and appreciate the extent of likely damage, which is key to any control efforts.

Be transparent: Everyone in the team must be transparent on the facts and truths of the situation at hand. Crises may be the time to support and be there for each other but not at the expense of telling the truths as they are. Transparency is both internal and external. Even if you will face regulators, good behaviour will earn you understanding, support and even concessions.

Move fast and move well: Damage control efforts must be fast and robust. You are better off with excess relief materials at the end than with shortages at the beginning or in the middle.

Seek help/Involve others! Quite often, we need help from within or outside organisations to solve an emerging crisis. The earlier we realise that and seek the required assistance, the faster we can resolve the challenge.

Resilience: Even in the best of times, an entrepreneur must be dogged. In crisis time, the entrepreneur must be resilient and clearheaded. There will be long days and sleepless nights, but the important thing to remember is that as long as you are doing the bits and pieces that are right, you will get to the end of the tunnel. Entrepreneurs are not known to give up unless that is the right thing to do. In times of crisis, there isn't any basis of giving up at all!

Post-crisis management and analysis: After the impact of a crisis is contained, the entrepreneur must continue to follow up with various functional supervisors as well as external parties until full normalisation is achieved. Even at that, reviews of production, finance and legal issues should continue with a view to ascertaining that any fallout consequences are further contained.

Post crisis analysis is about reviewing everything that has happened with a view to understanding any lapses and how they could have been avoided. It is about internally learning what could be done to avoid recurrence in the future.

30.0 Risk Management

Many budding entrepreneurs tend to think that business 'is about taking risk'. This is not a wise philosophy and may spell nothing but danger and pains. We should, therefore, try to understand exactly what risk is and how an entrepreneur should approach its understanding and management.

What is risk? From a business perspective, risk is simply the probability or call it the likelihood of an undesired event happening out of a number of possibilities. But beyond the *likelihood*, the *magnitude* of the unwanted consequence of the undesired event is another factor that is important in understanding risk and identifying, classifying, accepting, managing or mitigating it. For instance, for managerial purposes there is no risk if an undesired event is unlikely to occur or there is no unwanted consequence if the event does occur.

Transactions, projects and long-term businesses come with all sorts of risks. Some risks have zero unwanted or only little consequences that shouldn't bother us. We can live with those risks. But many other risks can severely hurt or even threaten the growth or even the survival of our businesses. We must understand those risks and take actions to mitigate them.

The importance of effective risk management: Effective risk management improves overall business processes, thereby protecting and enhancing the chances of business survival and growth.

When we manage risks well in our businesses, we are able to protect transactions, detect projects in trouble, take proactive actions and avoid catastrophic events. We improve communications within the organisation and our teams get focussed. Effective risk management reduces operational wastes and enhances our service delivery, revenues, cash flows and profitability. This engenders confidence in the business from all stakeholders, such as employees, customers, creditors and suppliers. All these will make business more stable, thereby improving the chances of further growth.

Types of risks: There are different types of risks, depending on your operating environment, industry, business model, business scale, location, etc. Sometimes even the specific timing and period within which a transaction is to be conducted may pose peculiar risks. Generally speaking, however, there are two types of risks, the internal and the external.

Internal risks are those risks that you may face or could even crystalise because of the internal weaknesses of your business. Internal risks include:

- Operational Risks: These are the risk of loss arising from inadequate or weak internal systems and processes. Operational risks could lead to other spinoff internal risks.

- Equipment risks: If you are running a manufacturing facility, you run the risk of old equipment failing, thereby resulting in downtimes, missed deliveries, etc. Any equipment risk that could cause unacceptable losses should be understood. In a service business, you may rely a lot on your computers and massive information. Any failure in the systems could spell disaster.

- Human risks: These are risks in business, which can arise as a result of the failure of your people to perform essentials tasks. They could also arise as a result of the fraudulent acts of sabotage by your people. Human risks may include illness, injuries or death of owner(s), resignation of key staff, etc.

- Financial risks: Financial risk refers to the possible effects on the flow of money in and out of your business. Increase in costs, delayed collection of receivables, etc. may lead to a business' cash flows not being sufficient to discharge its contractual obligations.

Typically, internal risks are easier to mitigate because they are almost entirely within your control. But it should also be noted that the crystallisation of one risk could trigger the likelihood of another. For instance, if your equipment fails to produce enough products, you may not be able to generate enough sales, thereby increasing your finance risks.

External risks, on the other hand, are risks that might crystallise as a result of actual the occurrence of external threats. They include:

- Political risks: Depending on your type of business, political risks can greatly affect your operations. This typically happens when there changes in government in developing countries even if the changes are democratic.

- Market risks: happenings in the marketplace can be volatile. You may not make the volume of sales you projected to make. You may also not be able to sell your products at the prices you projected. Any of such risks that could lower the value of your stock is a market risk.

- Environmental hazards: Flood, fire, etc. due to environmental factors outside our immediate control can cause damage and losses to our businesses. Depending specifically on what we do, we have to be alert to such risks and take preventative measures.

- Government and regulatory risks: This is the risk that a change in laws and regulations will materially impact your business, sector or market. Changes in regulations can increase the costs of operating a business. It may also serve as an incentive for potential competitors to come in thereby changing the competitive landscape.

There are a lot more specific risks that can impact on your business. These include compliance risks, legal risks, security risks, credit risks, cybersecurity risks, reputational risks, strategy risk, project risk, innovation risk, country or location risk, exchange rate risk, interest rate risk, seasonal risks, etc. Understanding risks is key to managing them.

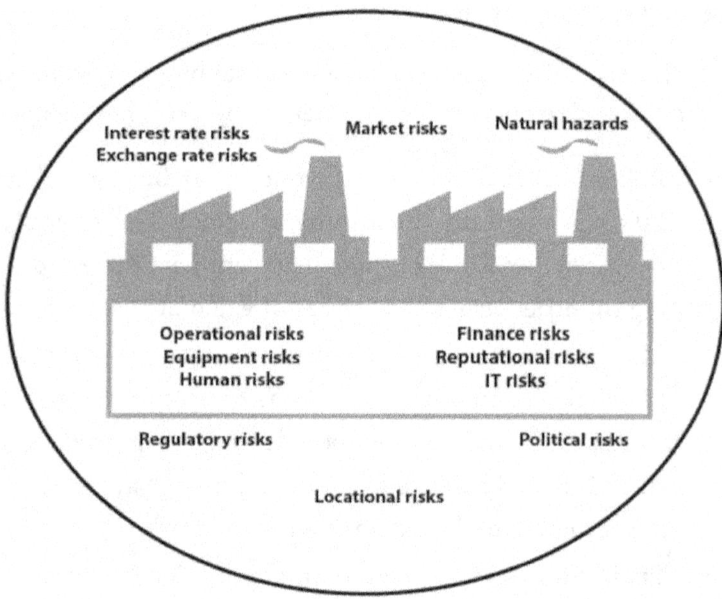

Figure 30.1: Some internal and external risks
(© Musbahu El Yakub)

What is risk management? Risk management refers to the deliberate processes of identifying and recognising risks, as well as developing methods to eliminate, minimize or manage them. This process involves:

- Risk identification
- Risk assessment (and prioritisation),
- Response development

Risks identification: The first thing to do in any risk management exercise is to identify risks. At this point, your concern should just be about those events the occurrence or lack of occurrence of which could cause disruptions or losses to the business.

If, for instance, you are to ship your perishable farm products from Kano to Lagos by road that will be paid for upon delivery, what are the likely events that could cause losses to your business on this transaction? What are the risks that the vehicle you hire to deliver the goods will break down on the road? What are the risks that the truck driver will spend days at a trailer rest stop without regards to the perishable nature of the goods? What are the risks that the vehicle could have an accident and the goods will be destroyed fully or partially?

Risk identification exercise should also include a good review and understanding of each risk is likely in the circumstance.

Risk assessment: Risk identification would only bring out all the risks that could impact on a specific transaction, project or business. Thereafter, you will need to assess each risk and rank it. Assessment and ranking are about establishing the likelihood of their occurrence and the negative consequences of their occurrence. A simple way is to start by assessing each event as 'very likely', 'moderately likely' or 'very unlikely'. Then rank them based on their likely negative impact on the business if they occur.

At this point, with an understanding of the risks, why they should be taken seriously and their ranking and likely magnitude, you will take up the important task of response development.

Response development: So far, you have identified each risk and assessed and ranked them. Now you will need to develop a response to each risk. Broadly speaking, there are three response options available to you:

- **Avoidance:** You can avoid a risk by eliminating its cause. If in a business there is a risk of theft of your stock from your warehouse, you may eliminate that risk by strengthening the physical security (manned, CCTVs, controlled access, etc.) as well as the processes of accessing the warehouse.

Risk avoidance is about taking a specific measure or measures to forestall the occurrence of the risk.

- **Mitigation:** This is about lowering the likely occurrence of the risk as well as managing the negative consequence of its crystallization. In the example of the delivery of perishables above, you could reduce the risks of losses on the road by employing the services of a reliable trucking company with a good fleet of trucks to try to reduce the risks of accidents and vehicle breakdown. In addition, you could cover your goods by a goods-in-transit insurance from a reputable insurance company, which will cover any losses that you may suffer if a breakdown or accident leads to the spoilage of the goods in whole or in part.

  Mitigation is sometimes about taking several measures to address just one risk or a group of risks. The example of the insurance is called *risk transfer*. Sometimes you could reduce your risk through *hedging, sharing, shifting,* etc.

- **Acceptance:** Sometimes a risk is identified as likely and there isn't much that could be done to avoid or mitigate it. In such a situation, you will need to assess if the likely consequences are bearable or hefty. If the likely consequence is bearable, that is easy to accept. If, on the other hand, the likely consequence is hefty, it will be to your calling to make a decision one way or the other.

- *Often, businessmen and decision makers accept risks with likely hefty consequences if they have done everything they could to minimise the likelihood of anything going wrong in a given situation. For instance, when NASA scientists and engineers decided to land man on the moon, they were very clear of the likely consequences of failing to return the astronauts back to Earth. But having done everything they needed to do, they accepted the risk which, thankfully, did not crystalise. We can, therefore, take risks IF we have done all that we can to satisfactorily minimise the likelihood of its occurrence.*

What are some of things you should do to ensure that your business is alert to the risks it faces and appropriate measures are always in place or can be put in place?

- Legal considerations: Ensure that your business is legally registered to do what it does. Renewals of certifications should be taken seriously and done timely to eliminate any windows in which you may operate outside by law by default. Retain a lawyer to provide such services, as may be required.

- Financial records: Keep your accounts properly and ensure that you make statutory payments as and when due. Retain an accountant to help you meet the various obligations.

- Employees: Make sure you have proper contracts with your employees. They should also be continuously trained well and motivated to keep them interested and committed to their jobs. If your staff are competent, they can sniff risks from a mile away and take care of them!

- Insurance: Identify all the areas of your business where insurance covers may be required either by law or just in your own business interests. Appropriate insurance can offer asset protection covers as well as against claims from third parties. Vehicles, office equipment, plant, etc. should all be insured. Goods-in-transit, fire, burglary and special perils should be covered depending on your situation and circumstances.

- Premises protection: This is particularly important when the location you operate is critical to your business. You should plan to have the rents, rates and any leases thereon paid on time to avoid disruptions.

- IT Systems: With growing significance of information technology in businesses, it is imperative that you take specific measures to protect your IT assets and secure the information you have. Make regular backups and ensure that you have at least one off-site backup,

- Customers: It is important you have deliberate measures to protect your business against the risks that customers could expose you to. You could, for instance, be forced out of business if you rely entirely on one or few customers. Customer and product diversification could shield you against that. Work to reduce the likelihood of dispute with you customers by having clear and upfront agreements. Credit risk issues should all be addressed,

- Vendors: As with customers, you should manage your vendor risk by procuring your supplies from a reasonable number of vendors. You should however be professional and upright by not divulging the confidential aspects of each relationship. Where appropriate and sensible, lock your vendors into long-term contracts,

- Service plans: Have service plans for the regular maintenance of your office and factory equipment. This is to reduce or eliminate the risk of breakdowns. Sometimes, it is necessary to include redundant assets at critical points in the office or the plant to eliminate certain risks.

- Put in place a monitoring system to ensure compliance, implementation and effectiveness of the detection, prevention and remedial action system.

- Different people have different risk affinities. Ensure that between you and your team you are able to balance your collective risk inclinations.

- Learn from those 'who have been there done that': Learning from others could save us all sorts of costs and headaches, and we should never fail to seize such opportunities. At the same time though, we should remain aware that learning from others is not about abdicating our responsibilities.

Managing risks is one of the key responsibilities you have to discharge diligently and competently to stand a chance to succeed in business. You have to take it seriously and develop the right culture of managing risks in your organisation.

31.0 Business Continuity Management

Things do go wrong in business, sometimes because of our failures to have done something right. Other times disasters are caused out of our control, such as by mother nature. Depending on the gravity of the incident, our business might suffer only mildly or hurt deeply. Unplanned disruptions of operations are the areas of interest of Business Continuity Management, which is our subject now.

In running a start-up factory with limited resources several years ago, we often had to get raw materials on credit from our suppliers. One of the major raw materials was palm-oil. On a particular day, we were able to get some one-hundred-and-twenty-thousand litres of the oil on credit. We were excited. The oil was stored in a cylindrical tank of several meters diametre that, for all intent and purposes, seemed physically stable on its feet that were hardly one foot each above the ground.

But early the following morning, I got a call from the factory about a major incident. I drove there at once to find our oil completely spilled out on the ground. Unrecoverable. In less than twelve hours, we had moved from having key stock that was to last us a few weeks to absolutely none of it. Our production had to shut down. In addition to that, we had an environmental clean-up challenge and a supplier to pay!

Businesses are vulnerable to catastrophes, such as accidental damages, wilful damage and natural disasters. Other times it is disasters at, say, our supply chain partner that may impact negatively on our own operations. Disasters range in timing, magnitude and impact. It may be a loss of laptop with all your business contacts, communication and information. It may be a farm that is completely submerged in flood. It could be loss of key staff, documents or millions of litres of oil spillage by a major oil company.

All sorts of errors, accidents and disasters do happen in business. Regardless of size, scope and operations, the budding entrepreneur should learn and adopt wise business continuity management practices to be able to handle unwanted disruptions as they arise with minimal negative consequences to the operations and reputation of the business.

What is Business Continuity Management? Business Continuity Management ('BCM') is the planning and preparation required to ensure that the likely occurrence of unwanted events is minimised and that a business maintains its functions or is able to quickly recover after unplanned disruption has occurred. It is a framework for identifying an organisation's exposure to internal and external threats and developing wise responses. The objective of BCM is to provide an organisation with the capacity to respond swiftly, deliberately and effectively to threats.

The benefits of BCM include:

- It mentally prepares operators on the likelihood of different disaster-types as well as exactly what should be done in the event of any disaster happening.

- Knowing what to do in advance of unwanted incident empowers operators and makes it possible for them to recover business operations quickly after disruptions.

- Mitigating risks strengthens an organisation and reduces actual costs of recovery in comparison to if there was no BCM framework in place.

- Effective BCM measures saves limbs, lives and money in the long run.

- Puts the organisation in compliance of regulatory requirements with positive consequences of the eliminated costs of litigations and claims.

- Earns business the confidence of host communities, customers and other stakeholders.

Business Continuity Planning: Specifically, Business Continuity Planning ('BCP') refers to the process of developing a system of identifying, eliminating and/or managing risks of disasters as well as handling the actual occurrence of disasters. A business continuity plan is a document developed to achieve the identified objectives of business continuity planning. It outlines how a business will manage and continue operations at the onset, during and after unplanned disruptions of operations.

There are three major components of BCP viz: Risk Assessment, Disaster Recovery and Restoration ('DRR') and Test, Approval and Implementation ('TAI') of the BCP.

Risks Identification and Assessment ('RIA'): The first thing to do is to identify specific company and sectoral risks as well as general business risks. Establish how each risk may affect different areas of your operations, as would have been outlined below.

Identifying Critical Assets and Business Functions: This is an impact analysis and management activity. It involves identifying critical business functions that must be maintained in a continuity situation in order to sustain operations and/or be in compliance with legal and moral requirements on the safety of lives and discharging contractual obligations. It also involves identifying critical assets and how they may be affected by different risks identified. How do you protect different assets and aspects of operations to different disruptions?

Other aspects of the planning that must be thought out include:

- **Internal and External Communication Procedures:** Communication with colleagues, customers, suppliers, regulators, etc. is key in difficult times. You should have a contacts' list and a clear channel of communication with different parties so as to be able to take appropriate actions to minimise damage from unplanned disruptions.

- **Alternate Supply Sources and Production:** Two critical business functions that suffer in many a continuity situation are supply chain and production capacities. Do you have buffer stock of raw materials and supplies that can keep you in safe production if an unplanned disruptive event takes place? Do you have alternate suppliers that can deliver raw materials to you if your major supplier is in a continuity situation themselves and unable to meet your orders?

Four more important aspects of business continuity planning are:

- **Orders of Succession:** A business continuity plan should be clear about succession hierarchies. For instance, who should act for the managing director if the managing director is incapacitated or unavailable, for any reason, during a continuity period? Who should act for the marketing manager if the marketing manager is unavailable during a continuity period? Similarly, all other key positions must have successors that have the full powers and authority of the substantive but unavailable official until the latter resumes.

- **Plan Activation and Deactivation:** There should also be a clear activation and deactivation of procedures of the continuity plan. This is about what specific incidents will prompt the activation of the plan and what achievements will trigger plan deactivation. Who should activate (and deactivate) the continuity plan? How should the activation (and deactivation) be communicated?

- **Plan Reviews:** A business continuity plan has a life of its own determined by a validity period as well as other exigencies. Consequently, it must be reviewed from time to time either because it has 'expired' or because there are fundamental changes in operational risks and/or other issues that need to be incorporated in the plan.

- **Document the Plan:** Regardless of the size of your operation, it is necessary that the plan is formalised in a document. There are available simple and free templates that will serve the purpose of even small operations. They help you to think through the issues in a methodical manner.

The two other major components of business continuity planning process are as follows:

Disaster Recovery and Restoration ('DRR'): The ultimate objective of every business continuity plan is a quick, effective and efficient recovery from disaster and restoration to normal operations from unplanned interruptions. The purpose of disaster recovery and restoration activities is to ensure that you are able to assess the extent of interruption, identify what human and other resources are required for quick recovery and restoration and how all those resources can be mobilised.

This stage of the planning process will, consequently, include the use of pre-identified communication channels, deployment of key personnel, provision of raw materials, etc. Your DRR strategy is to aim at providing a capacity for quick but detailed disaster assessment, communication between individuals and with units and other organisations, assignment of individual and team responsibilities and provision of the resources required to restore back to normalcy.

A specific element of disaster recovery and restoration that is particularly critical is communication between key staff and also with suppliers, customers, your external engineers, regulators, etc. Having a contacts list of all key stakeholders and operators is integral to this part of the plan.

Test, Approval and Implementation ('TAI'): As the name suggests, this is the stage at which three integrated subcomponents of the plan are carried out.

- **Test the Plan:** The first subcomponent involves developing testing criteria as well as procedures. How well are the components of the plan coordinated? How easily can procedures be carried out? At the end of this stage, you have to be comfortable that your plan is executable.

- **Approval:** This is the stage at which the test results are reviewed and approved if they meet the set objectives. Whist the approval itself is an executive management responsibility, the opinions and suggestions of operatives should be taken into consideration.

'Renewals' and 'maintenance' are two important aspects of this process. At the end of a pre-set period, the plan must be reviewed and reapproved to ensure that it remains in line with strategic goals, current and valid. Similarly, when certain fundamentals change, the plan should be reviewed to ensure that alignment is maintained.

- **Implementation:** Once the plan is approved, it should be available to those that should have it. Those to carry out specific aspects of the plan should be trained to be able to do so proficiently.

Below is a schematic representation of the three major components of business continuity planning and how they relate with each other:

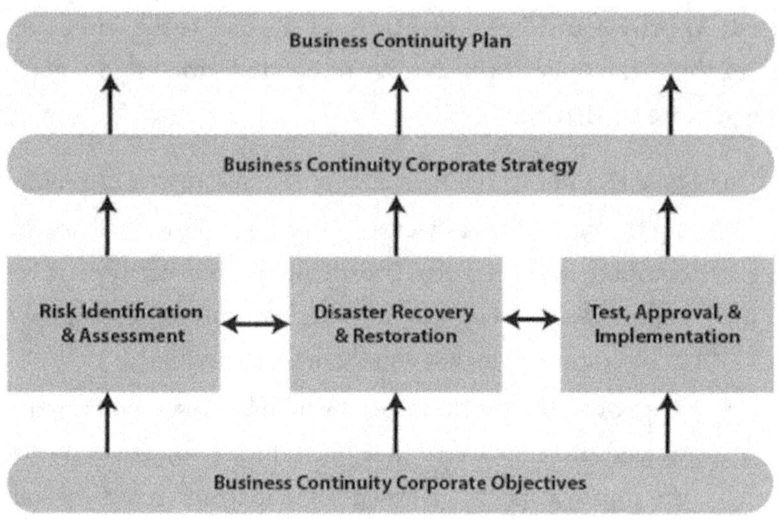

Figure 31.1: Components of Business Continuity Management
(© Musbahu El Yakub)

Irrespective of your type and size of business, you and your team should think through and come up with a business continuity plan that will meet your requirements. For large corporations, business continuity plans are sophisticated and detailed documents that must take into consideration not only some of the factors that we discussed here but also others, such as diversity, time zones, multi-locations, multi-operations, etc. For the entrepreneur, you just need some document that is simple but workable and effective. Thinking through the issues and writing them down will force you into developing solutions to problems that will work and can save your business in difficult times.

32.0 Business Growth Planning

The desire for continuous business growth comes naturally for most entrepreneurs. However, growing a business requires wise planning to create and seize growth opportunities while also avoiding pitfalls and dangers. The careful planning of business growth is our subject over the next pages.

Business growth planning defined: Business growth may be measured by several metrics, such as increase in sales revenue, profitability, number of employees, number of customers, product diversification, number of branches, increase in fixed assets, etc. The process of developing a business growth plan that may be required to achieve certain growth measures is called business growth planning. The product of a growth planning activity is a business growth plan, which is a strategic framework that guides the growth of a business or part thereof from one stage to another over a period.

The importance of growth planning: Planning for growth is crucial in ensuring that every action taken is meant specifically towards achieving carefully desired and chosen growth targets. This helps to focus all efforts and makes possible the optimum allocation and use of resources. Consequently, goals are achieved with minimum wastage of resources while at the same time maximum possible value is created. The process of business growth planning helps the entrepreneur and their management in thinking afresh and being more creative. It also brings about the additional need for accountability in what is to be done and how it will be done.

Furthermore, employees who are aware of business growth objectives and plans are more disposed to working towards achieving them than those that are not. Stakeholders, such as shareholders, are able to monitor the actual progress made vis-à-vis projected targets. Similarly, financiers can also assess the extent of financial resources that may be required to achieve growth targets and whether or not the projected levels of financing are sufficient, bloated or inadequate.

Business growth trajectory: To plan for growth, it is essential to understand the typical growth trajectory of most businesses and where your business is presently positioned. Generally, five stages are identified as those of 'Existence', 'Survival', 'Success', 'Take-off' and 'Resource Maturity'. A more detailed depiction by Harvard Business Review captures the differences in 'Management style', 'Organisation', 'Extent of formal systems', 'Major strategy', and relationship between 'Business and owner' in each of those stages.

I like to see those stages in terms of the size, age, market potentials and capacity as well as the position of a business in a market. A caveat, though, is that growth is non-linear because different businesses, led by different leaders, can grow differently, often jumping stage(s). Similarly, stagnation, decline and ultimate death could also happen at any stage, albeit differently, for different possible causes. This means that even as opportunities and threats might differ, each business at each stage can prosper and stabilise for a while or grow further. Consequently, it is necessary that the entrepreneur is aware of the challenges and opportunities at each stage and know what can be done to address the challenges and seize the opportunities.

Elements of a business growth plan: There are five important elements of a business growth plan. These are the *specific goals* to be achieved, the *timeframe* over which a desired growth is to be achieved, the *resources* to be provided, the *specific actions* to be taken to ensure that set targets are achieved from one stage to another and the *assignment of officers and units* to specific duties to be discharged.

Types of growth: The growth pathway to be taken by a business will depend on the personal dispositions, preferences and capacities of the entrepreneur and managers as well as the opportunities and constraints in the environment, the resources available to and for deployment by the business, etc. Regardless of these factors though, you could grow your business along the following broad possibilities:

- **Organic** – Where the business reinvests its internally available resources to achieve more through capacity expansion. This is sometimes called internal growth.

- **Strategic** – This is a long-term growth approach through which specific initiatives are carried out, for instance, to gain share in a market that was hitherto unconsidered and therefore untapped.

- **Partnerships** – This is a pathway to growth through which a business partners/merges with or acquires other(s) to create more market opportunities.

The type of business growth pathway to be taken is a critical issue that should not be taken lightly.

Growth strategies: There are various growth strategies that an entrepreneur could adopt for their business. These include:

- Improving efficiency: One of the first pathways to growth we should always look to is the enhancement of our productivity and efficiency in everything we do. Cutting out wastes and getting more done with existing resources can achieve growth mileage for us.

- Market penetration: Market penetration is about creating further growth in the same market. This means we should strive to sell more of our product in the same market. There are two possibilities here: Selling more to the same customers or getting new customers that are either not taken or away from your competitors!

- New product development: This is about creating new products to generate more revenue. This is one of the most difficult and risky ways of achieving growth but could also be the most rewarding if you get things right.

- Market expansions: To achieve growth through market expansions, you try to reach new markets with your existing products. It could, for instance, be through geographic expansions.

- Integrations: Vertical integration is a growth strategy through which you take control of more stages of your sourcing, production and distribution. This could mean you begin to produce your packages, which you probably used to buy from suppliers. Horizontal integration, on the other hand, involves the acquisition of other companies or assets in the same business line. That means, for instance, if you are producing soaps, you acquire another company that is producing soaps as well.

So far, we have defined what business growth planning is, its importance, business growth trajectory, the elements of growth planning, types of growths and growth strategies. We can now take up how to plan for growth in your business.

Growth is holistic: Whilst what we have been discussing is generally about overall corporate growth, there are also functional growths. For instance, a growth plan could be limited to a specific function, such as marketing or production. This is possible when one function has to 'catch up' with another, or one functional growth could just serve as the 'driver' for an overall desired corporate growth to be achieved. Just like in living organisms, growth in a business is also holistic. This means planning for growth in a business must take all the factors associated with the business into consideration. For instance, any plan to quadruple your sales and triple your profitability in five years would influence and be influenced by your production capacity, staff strength, increase in working capital requirements, etc. So, even when you plan for growth in a specific business function, like production, you have to take into account the impact of the increase in your production capacity on your marketing, finance, human resource management, etc.

Business growth planning: As mentioned earlier, there are different stages and types of growth. Regardless of the type of the growth scope and strategy, the plan development processes are the same. They include:

- **Establish where you are:** The first thing to do in growth planning is to establish where you currently are. This includes evincing your current production capacity, sales volume and revenue, staff strength, current assets and specifically working capital capacity, etc.

- **Assess the opportunities you have:** Whatever growth objectives you want to achieve cannot be decided blindly. Rather, you will need to assess the opportunities that you can seize as well as the challenges that you may be facing. Opportunities might be in the market with your existing products to existing customers. It could be with existing products to new customers. Similarly, there could be opportunities that could be derived from your 'excess' production capacity or simply from your massive cash holdings. Other than opportunities, sometimes growth can be achieved just by addressing challenges! For instance, you may already have a lot of room for growth in your existing market but are constrained by insufficient working capital. In such a situation, addressing your working capital constraints can springboard you to desirable growth targets. But even in such situations, your planning must remain holistic.

Establishing opportunities available to you is fundamental to your growth planning process.

- **Establish your growth objectives:** At this stage, you define what goals you want to achieve at clearly defined milestones. Your goals should be 'SMART' as in 'specific', 'measurable', 'achievable', 'relevant' and 'time-bound'. A growth target must be backed by several metrics that can be measured along timelines. A target might be, for instance, to quadruple your sales and triple your profitability in five years, as mentioned earlier. All other metrics that support the achievement of these objectives, such as a specific increase in number of staff and increase in working capital, must also be established.

- **Identify and provide required resources:** For the target you aspire to achieve, you have to identify if you already have the required resources. If you do not, you have to plan to have them provided. Resources might include additional working capital and a number of sales staff, as mentioned previously. Whatever the additional and required resources, you have to plan to provide them when they are needed.

- **Assign responsibilities:** After establishing what your targets are, you have to assign the people and units that will be responsible for which actions and which targets within the time windows set. The responsible individuals and units should be clear of what is expected of them, when and, perhaps, how. They should also be provided the resources they require as mentioned earlier.

- **Set clear timelines and action plans:** For each growth target you wish to achieve, you will need to identify which actions are necessary to be carried out, at what time and by whom.

- **Stakeholders meeting:** All stakeholders should be involved in agreeing the with targets to aspire for. Once such goals are agreed upon and resources provided, a regular stakeholder meeting should periodically hold. The idea is to ensure that you remain on track and any issues and problems are addressed as they arise. These meetings will be about the rigorous supervision of implementation and adjustments wherever and whenever necessary.

- **Watch out for pitfalls:** Working towards your growth targets will not be easy. There may be issues of resource constraints, perhaps human capital challenges, economic downturns, etc. Whatever the challenges, you have to be able to rework and adjust your plans and implementation while remaining focussed on your targets. Sometimes, however, situations might necessitate changes and amendments in targets. This can be both desirable and legitimate.

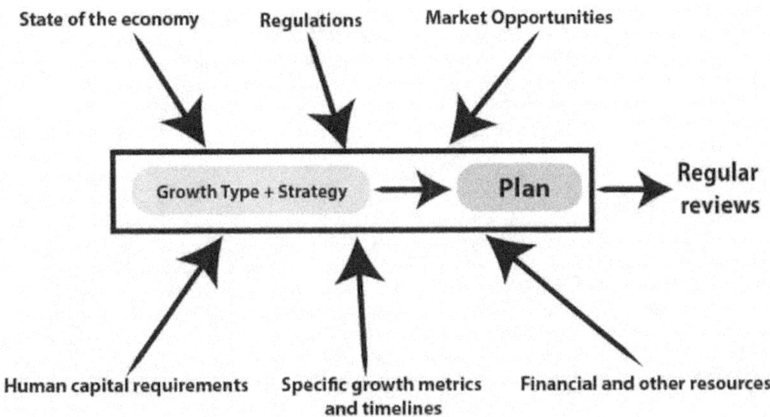

Figure 32.1: Elements of a growth plan
(© Musbahu El Yakub)

As a consultant, I have always used the criteria of room for growth to advise on which businesses entrepreneurs should get into and which to avoid. Businesses without room for growth will not be interesting over the long run for most entrepreneurs.

33.0 Business Performance Review

The only way to know if you are making progress in your business and/or if there are problems is by conducting regular business performance reviews, which shall be our subject now.

When I first started out on the path of entrepreneurship, I began with a computer parts import business even while I was still a private sector employee. Every last weekend of the month I sat down with a freelance agent, who was my salesman, to review the transactions of the month. We worked out the profitability of the month's transactions and where there was any loss we immediately absorbed it and continued with our lives. We drew up the statement of affairs as at the end of the month, which showed us what we had in inventory, receivables, cash, any liabilities, etc. That monthly performance review exercise was one of the most exciting things I was doing at that time. I could clearly see how the business was growing on a monthly basis. Problems were immediately resolved and opportunities explored.

You can only know how well you are doing, what problems you will need to resolve and what opportunities you can seize further by reviewing your business performance regularly and diligently.

What is businesses performance review? Your business must have objectives, benchmarks and budgets against which you can compare with actual performance of its various components and the performance of the business overall at the point of assessment as well as over past periods. A fundamental responsibility for entrepreneurs and their management staff is a regular review of the state of the business. Business performance review is the assessment of the actual commercial and non-commercial effectiveness and efficiency of a business as its board, management and staff strive to achieve pre-set desired objectives.

The importance of business performance review: It is quite tempting to get bogged down by the daily grinds of running a business. While this is necessary for the operational success of a business, an entrepreneur can get weighed down by them, leading to loss of focus on strategic visioning and planning.

A regular business performance review is required to ascertain how the health of the business as well what strengths can be further leveraged on. A performance review will also bring out the weaknesses that may need to be addressed. Performance review is not just about the performance of the business as a whole, but also the performance of component units and even individuals within the business. These details are required for improvement in individual, unit, and overall corporate performance.

Performance reviews make it possible for you to sharpen your plans and strategies going into the future. It helps you to identify specific areas that need improvements, such as increasing inventory turnover, lowering certain costs, delivering better customer services, etc. In-depth performance reviews will help you to optimise the allocation of resources and improve your business efficiency in the use of finances and production assets.

What are the components of a business performance review? Your review sessions are opportunities for you to further understand the details of your business as well as its operating environment. This suggests that your review will include:

- **Understanding the macro-environment:** Every business operates within some socio-economic and political environment. Your business is impacted by both global and local factors. Understanding the constraints and opportunities within these environments is necessary if you are to make a success of it.

- **Assess your business performance vis-a-vis your targets and objectives:** You should always have a projection of what you want to achieve in sales revenue, gross profit margins, various ratios of overheads accounts to sales, productivity metrics for individual staff, units and functions, etc. Periodic performance review will then make it possible for you to see how well you are doing in comparison to your own targets. This is required if you are to be able to take intelligent remedial actions, as may be required.

- **Assess your position in the competitive landscape:** Your performance reviews will enable you to benchmark what you are achieving against industry averages and against major competitors. The result should help you further sharpen your strategies or alter them altogether.

What do you review? Basically, you can review anything and everything of importance at a performance review meeting. However, we can group the issues broadly on the following:

- **Economic and social environments:** All businesses operate within a local and global economy. What is happening globally and locally? How do they impact your business, positively or negatively? What can you do better? What is happening in your local politics, are there elections coming up and how do they impact on your business?

- **Assessment of core activities:** This includes issues of product performances and customer responses, which products are doing best in what areas, etc.

- **Assessment of business efficiency:** This is about how efficiently resources are used to achieve results. What is the capacity utilisation of the machines that you have? What is your inventory turnover? etc.

- **Review of financial performance:** What is your turnover? Why is it what it is? How is your dynamic cash flow position? How good are your working capital management ratios? If you are leveraged, how able are you to service the interest component and make any principal repayments?

- **Understanding the customer:** Understanding the customer and delivering what they expect is key to your competitive strength and market position (below). Are there any changes in customers' needs and expectations? Are there new and emerging services? Who is introducing them to the customers?

- **Competition and market analysis:** What market share do you have, is it growing or shrinking? Who are your competitors, how are they doing? What are they doing better than you? What competitive advantages do you have or do they have? Can you protect the advantages you have?

- **Staff and unit performances:** How the various units in your business and the individual staff doing?

Figure 33.1: Business performance review
(© Musbahu El Yakub)

How do you review your business performance? Your performance review exercise is always about assessing your actual performance against what you have budgeted/planned to do and perhaps benchmark against what others are doing or what can be achieved. This means:

- **People:** You must have the right team to capture all the information and be able to review the performance of the business. The 'team' might just be you at some point when you are starting out or along with a part-time staff like my sales agent when I was selling computer components. As you grow, you may need performance reviews at individual, unit and of course corporate levels. To do this, you need the people that understand business and its measures of success.

- **Information:** The people you have can only review the business performance if certain information is available. The first document required document is the performance report. The objective is to match the actual performance against the budgeted plan. Variances should also be captured to understand them, what caused them and what can be done whether they are positive or negative. With modern computers and applications, it is now easy to have all the report that we need to assess how well our businesses are doing.

- **It is not only numbers:** Your performance reviews should not be limited to financials and other 'numbers'. You should also discuss other issues like your operating structure, staff motivation, strategy, etc.

- **Timing:** The frequency of your performance reviews will depend on your type of business, size and the people that must participate, etc. What is important is that it must be regular and frequent. Enough window should, however, be given to people to achieve significant components of their targets but must not be too wide for people to rest on their oars. Even if you are the only one to conduct it, be regular and religious about it. Individuals and units could review their performances weekly while at the corporate level it could be monthly or quarterly, again depending on your size and the seniority of the people to be involved. Regardless, the least is a quarterly review and also on annual basis.

- **Planning forward:** In the review of your past performance, you should also keep planning ahead. This means as you assess what you have achieved, you could choose to keep your budget as it is or you could choose to review it upwards or even downwards. Whatever it is you are doing must be based on intelligent and credible new information and/or realities and should be in the overall interest of the business and its stakeholders.

- **Conduct:** Many officials are apprehensive of a performance review meetings. They expect it to be hostile and condescending where they are dressed down for failures. Consequently, they adopt a defensive attitude to it. This is quite unnecessary and can be avoided by the wise entrepreneur.

Ensure that you create an amiable atmosphere and encourage your people to understand that performance a review is about each person, unit and the organisation doing the best. Where people and units fall short, they should be encouraged and supported to improve even if they are held responsible.

- **Preparation:** Participants of a business performance review must prepare in advance of their presentations. Documents, expect those for limited and restricted circulations, should be shared to those who need to review them ahead of the meeting. Participants must be encouraged to review those documents in advance for fruitful discussions.

- **Engagement:** It is important that the entrepreneur leads the performance review as an intellectually stimulating and business exciting activity through rigour, detail and depth. The kind of questions you will be asking and must be getting answers at a performance review will include:

  o What were our targets in various units and overall? What were the actual achievements?

  o What were the variances and what caused them?

  o Are our assets being efficiently utilised in all spheres of our activities?

  o Could we have done better? Why? Why didn't we? How can we?

  o What (factors) and who (individuals and groups) were essentially responsible for meeting or surpassing any targets? What did they do right?

  o What can the organisation do to leverage on the successes further? Take a note here to ensure that the organisation learns and internalises the factors that caused successes. This can be done by putting measures that will reinforce the behaviours that caused the success, etc.

  o What were the challenges, setbacks, 'near misses' and failures? What factor(s) was/were responsible for them? What wasn't done right?

o   Was there any particular person or group that was fundamentally responsible for them? This should however not be a blame apportionment exercise, but an opportunity to learn and avoid recurrence,

o   What have the individuals, groups and the organization at large learnt from the failure?

o   What has been done and/or can be done, in the future, to eliminate the risk that caused the failure?

o   What was done to reverse the negative situations? Who was responsible? What can be done to reward them and reinforce such behaviour in the organisation?

o   Do you need to adjust (upwards or downwards) your targets in light of current realities and developments?

A business performance review is an absolute must activity that should hold regularly and without fail. It helps your people, you and your organisation to remain focused, diligent and result-oriented.

34.0 Responsible Corporate Citizenship

An interesting feature of success, which many do not realise, is that it is more about other people than it is about the successful individual. Think about it: A company that makes a billion Naira profit might share a part of that profit to shareholders. But before the profit was made, customs clearing agents were paid their fees for clearing the raw materials of the company at the port; suppliers of fuels were paid; staff salaries were paid; transporters delivering goods from the factory to the customers were paid, etc. The customs clearing agents employ other people, the transporters patronise food sellers on the way to delivery, staff pay school fees at private institutions that their children attend, etc. The point is the more successful we may be, the more others benefit from us and what we do in so many more ways than we may directly benefit. This should not only be clear to us, but we must be excited about and embrace it. But over and above paying customs agents for their services, staff for their salaries and transporters for their services also, we need to make our businesses responsible corporate citizens. How do we go about that?

What is corporate citizenship? By law, corporations are legal entities with several human-like features, rights and responsibilities. Unfortunately, many entrepreneurs focus only on the economic goals of running their businesses. But beyond revenues and profitability, entrepreneurs should also be aware and alive to their legal, ethical and even voluntary social responsibilities. Corporate citizenship is about the responsibilities that a business owes the society. The ultimate objective of responsible corporate citizenship is about helping to deliver higher standards of living and the quality of life for communities in which the business operates directly or indirectly.

In a paper on Nigeria's financing of healthcare during the Covid-19 pandemic, it was reported that a total of US$560.52 million, about N213 billion then, was collected in Nigeria as at 13th July, 2020. Of *the collected amount, more than ninety per cent was made by private sector donors. The financial and non-financial contributions of the private sector to various developmental efforts, from local communities to national levels, are what we must continue to provide for the upliftment of our societies and grow as entrepreneurs.*

What are the benefits of responsible corporate citizenship? The purpose of all responsible corporate citizenship efforts is for an entrepreneur and their business to positively contribute to people, communities and societies. The activities you conduct could also be tax deductible and you and your corporation will earn a lot of goodwill from the government as well as communities. Beyond all that, you and your staff will derive satisfaction in the services that you provide beyond personal economic benefits. In addition, your social activities will give your brand better recognition as well as greater organizational growth through goodwill and patronage.

There are conditions for responsible corporate citizenship:

1. Legitimacy of activities: All activities you will be engaged in must be sanctioned by the law.
2. Protect the environment: The activities you engage in should protect the environment. Where necessary, environmental impact assessments must be conducted before actions are taken.

How do you make your business a responsible corporate citizen? The International Organisation for Standardisation (ISO) has developed a set of standards that can help in the implementation of corporate social responsibility by companies. But I have a slightly different pathway that I like to suggest as follows:

1. **Yes, again start from mind!** You will need to first understand the deep positive implications of the contributions you are likely to make as being worthy of all the effort and

resources you may put in and the sacrifices you may make. You then have to internalise that and also carry along your people.

2. **Establish your areas of engagements:** Identify the areas of engagement in which your company has the capacity in terms of competence and resources, as well as the needs of the community, communities or causes you want to support. At this stage, it is pertinent that you commit to only what you can sustain. Interestingly, we should understand that people appreciate our intentions and commitment more than the actual quantum of our interventions. So, it is advisable that you start modestly even as you look into the future with more ambitious programs.

3. **Understand where best you can help:** The process of establishing your areas of possible engagements involves studying the areas of the needs of the communities and causes you wish to support. This will involve talking directly with stakeholders, who may include individuals and communities, as well as other businesses, government agencies and non-governmental organisations. Similarly, you will need to develop internal policies on exactly what you will do and how you will do them. Focus on the results you want to achieve should remain clear.

4. **Set up a system:** Carrying out interventions well requires that you build a system. Beyond the policies mentioned above, you should identify units and officials and the responsibilities they are to discharge and how to discharge them. Whatever system you put in place must include a continuous assessment of the impact of your interventions.

5. **Spend wisely:** The whole idea of your interventions is about improving the standards of living, the quality of life and creating opportunities. Consequently, you should be prudent through ensuring that every Naira you invest will achieve or contribute to the achievement of your set objectives.

6. **Encourage innovation and participation:** Solving problems and creating solutions is about innovation. The participation of people of different statuses, experiences and backgrounds does help in creating solutions. Encourage your people, the beneficiaries, and experts to participate and contribute in what you are trying to do.

Our business successes are not just about our turnover, profitability and the personal good lives that we enjoy. Ultimate business success is also about our positive impact to the public and our communities beyond what may be our legal responsibilities. We can contribute to communities and charity groups in small and not-so-small-ways. We can be partners in running a local orphanage or support a local public primary school with supplies or finance the university education of brilliant but indignant students, etc.

Our social contributions to our communities beyond our economic roles are great indicators of our humanity and true success. Let us take and play this role as committedly as we take our economic responsibilities.

35.0 Business Exits and Succession Planning

Most entrepreneurs in Africa tend to think that once they start a business they are 'stuck' with it for life. Whilst some people spend decades in the same business for quite legitimate and valid reasons, it is possible to leave a business at some point in time for equally legitimate and valid reasons. There are several reasons why we may leave our businesses. Irrespective of the reasons, we should plan our departures well.

Business exits and succession planning: Whilst entrepreneurs tend to be highly committed, even emotionally attached, to their business, it helps to have exit options pre-planned. Exit options might be for several reasons, such as voluntary retirement or disengagement due to health or legal reasons. Exits could also be because you sell the business in whole or in part. Succession planning, on the hand, is about gradual handover to successor over a period within which the successor or successors are gradually groomed to be capable to taking the business to the next level.

When exit options, including succession, are pre-planned, deliberate strategies are developed that will make transition smooth and with minimum rancour and disruptions beyond what is required.

There are quite a few options of exiting a business fully or partially. Whatever options you may decide to take, it is important you engage the right professionals before, during and after the option is carried out. Some of the exit options include:

Initial public offering: One of the best ways to divest from a business is through an initial public offering (IPO). This is about selling shares of your company under various possible options and taking it public for the first time. Depending on your shareholding and local regulation, you may or not be able to divest all your shareholding while taking your company to the stock market.

Partially for fully selling out is often a very profitable way of cashing out if you have created substantial value and your company valuation comes out high.

Strategic mergers and acquisitions: Another option of exiting fully or partially is actually to merge your business with another business or businesses either to 'walk away' or remain in some capacity. Merging with another business could mean you remain a shareholder of the larger/new business but may or may not be involved in the management or board directioning, depending on the terms of the deal.

Like the IPO mentioned earlier, you can profitably cash out if you have created good value and are able to create a good fit between merging or with acquiring firms.

Management buyouts: Sometimes, the management of a business could buy out the owner(s) of a business, who walk away and the management become the new owners. In most cases, this happens when the management has more confidence in the prospects of the company than its shareholders. However, shareholders could also sell out to management if the former are happy with the offer by the latter.

Sell a part or whole of the business: As much as possible, selling a business, in part or in whole, should be at a time when you have already created sufficient value and can get an excellent valuation for the worth of the business or part of it that you will be selling. Typically, you could sell to your partner(s), new external shareholders. Regardless of who might be buying, what is important is that the valuation should be fair, reasonable and good for you.

Strip and liquidate the assets: If you have not created value that will attract a wholesale pricing that makes sense, you could opt to strip and liquidate your assets to those who will pay a premium for the bits and pieces rather than the whole. Depending on what you have on ground and the state of the economy, this option generally takes time to fully pan out. Consequently, you have to cut down on your overheads within the wait out period, so that they don't eat into the sales proceeds you may be collecting. Similarly, you have to ensure the provision of security and a detailed records of the assets that you will be stripping.

Each sale of an asset or assets must be fully documented. Keep copies of original ownership documents. When discussing terms of sales, it is often appropriate to make them on 'as is' basis even if, say, equipment are fully functional and in good condition.

Depending on your business type and regulatory requirements on it, the process of selling it can be easy or complicated. But whatever it may be, it is appropriate that you engage the necessary consultants, such as accountants, lawyers, corporate finance advisors, etc. Full disclosures are necessary and term sheet must capture all the details of the agreement. You do not want to sell and be dragged back into litigations.

Handing over to family or management staff: It also happens that entrepreneurs wish to hand over to family successors for one of several possible reasons. Maybe the entrepreneur wishes to hand over to a family member due to health reasons, old age or because the family member or members have come of age and can run the affairs of the business satisfactory. Whatever might be the trigger, it is important that a proper succession plan is developed and diligently carried out. This should involve:

- A selection of a few possible candidates from the family.
- Putting the candidates through development programs on and off the job over a reasonable period of time.

In the event that you wish to hand over to a member of your management staff, you should train them over a good a period.

Regardless of to who succession is being planned, documentation in fundamental. When family members are involved, you should do everything possible to clarify issues and generally smoothen any rough edges.

Planned business exits and successions are important for the smooth transition from one management team to another. It demonstrates good corporate governance practices.

36.0 The Traits of Successful Entrepreneurs

"Nothing ventured. Nothing gained."
– Old adage

I could have presented this at the beginning of the book. But I kept it to the last because having gone through the book, this will be easier appreciated by the reader at this point.

First, we should understand that entrepreneurs come in different 'colours, shapes and sizes'. Other than a few core characteristics, there just isn't a 'one size fits all'. Entrepreneurs are influenced individually by their upbringing, environment, personal desires and preferences, education, travels around the world, their businesses, risk profiles, etc. However, a few characteristics are common to most.

They love what they do and they work hard: Successful entrepreneurs truly love what they do. I think it is the only way to succeed in tough environments. The love for what entrepreneurs do gives them the passion for it and the passion for it generates commitment. The intensity of their commitment makes it 'easy' for them to put in the hard work and the long hours that they need to succeed. Issues will crop up at 'wrong' times and 'wrong' days, but they must be attended to anyway. Interestingly, entrepreneurs may start a business they initially didn't necessarily love. However, the success they achieve can, over time, makes them love the business they are engaged in.

Successful entrepreneurs have a great work ethic and are highly disciplined. They, particularly, understand the imperative to make a good use of their time and other resources towards achieving their objectives. The love for what they do and the willingness to work hard make it easy for them to be biased for action, which is an absolute must for success.

Confident and Resilient: Entrepreneurs generally have high a level of confidence. That is not to say that they live in some dream world devoid of reality. On the contrary, they are internally realistic. They understand that though what they are trying to achieve may be a stretch of what seems impossible to others, they have three things on their minds that make them comfortable. First, they have a very clear *vision* of the objective they want to achieve; second, they have some *road map*, even if initially broad, that they plan to follow; and third, they are willing *to raise and commit the required resources*. Friends and relations, who really mean well to you, will cast doubt on what you want to do. You have to remain realistic, positive and focused in the midst of doubt, fear and even distractions.

Successful entrepreneurs are amazingly resilient. They hardly give up when they are in pursuit of some commercial objectives. When they do give up, it is usually not because they cannot continue but because giving up is probably the technically right and pragmatic thing to do.

They thrive in the face of challenges: Things inclining to go wrong in life are almost a natural tendency in our real world. In addition, the more things you try to do, the more things are likely to go wrong. This means entrepreneurs are, unsurprisingly, confronted with many issues at any point in time. It may be trying to meet a delivery deadline, making a payroll, a major customer getting delinquent in payment, poor cash flow, an accident at the factory, etc. all at the same time! No one likes problems, but entrepreneurs are always willing to face challenges as they arise. This is necessary if they are to succeed in the competitive environment they choose to operate in.

They manage risks: Contrary to the popular belief that entrepreneurs are 'risk takers', the reality is that successful entrepreneurs are aware of the risks they are taking in any given transaction, project or endeavour. First, they are able to identify the risks. Second, they assess the likelihood of any of the risks that may crystalise. Third, they try to understand the magnitude of the loss that may be suffered if a particular risk crystalises. Based on these three, they then put in measures to completely eliminate or mitigate the likely occurrence and/or consequence(s) of specific risk(s). In some cases, some risks simply can't either be eliminated or fully mitigated. So, the typical entrepreneur will decide whether or not they can 'live' with the consequences of the identified risk if it does crystalise. This is where individual 'risk inclinations' and the 'risk profile' of different entrepreneurs come into play. The entrepreneur then makes a call and doesn't look back.

Resolve to win and the willingness to fail: Successful entrepreneurs always start on a resolve to win. That is why they work hard and commit resources. That is why they are highly competitive. That is why they hardly give up simply because something is 'difficult'. Whenever they seem to be 'at the end of the road' on an issue, successful entrepreneurs come up with ideas to open up more roads on their journey. Interestingly, successful entrepreneurs are also willing to fail. The mindset of the successful entrepreneur is inclined towards 'I would rather try and fail' than 'I wouldn't try lest I fail!'

Resourceful, Creative and Innovative: Successful entrepreneurs are great learners. Every interaction is considered an opportunity to learn something new. They listen to experts and experienced people, and are just generally receptive to new and credible information and knowledge. They need all that because they must be resourceful, creative and innovative in coming up with solutions to problems if they are to succeed in. They task themselves and think outside the box to develop new ideas and lines of action.

They are emotionally intelligent: Successful entrepreneurs are self-aware and can also understand others. That is why they generally tend to have great, even if exacting, leadership qualities that are result-focussed and result-oriented. They are self-motivated without the need for others to push them. They are great self-leaders always conscious of what they should do and what they should not do in different scenarios. Great entrepreneurs are decisive and yet flexible in dealing with others and handling situations.

They nurture relationships: To succeed in business, you need to understand and build core relationships. Having a supportive family relationship really helps. It makes otherwise difficult endeavours easier to handle. Building great teams is a definite must if you are to succeed as an entrepreneur. But there are also other circles of relationships that must also be built, nurtured and protected. Other entrepreneurs, trade associations and groups of professional advisors, such as bankers, lawyers, etc. must be cultivated by you. To succeed as an entrepreneur, you need to build your core tribe. And 'tribe' here doesn't mean your narrow ethnic stock. Rather, it means a group of core people that are always there for you in the course of your pursuit but who also must benefit in some ways from you and your endeavours. This tribe tends to be relatively stable over time, but as you grow in entrepreneurship, it is likely to also grow and some individuals are likely to fall by the roadside.

What needs to be understood, however, is that great entrepreneurship is not necessarily about out-of-the-world financial achievements. Whilst that might be a part of the success metric for the entrepreneur, what you do and how you do it are equally indicators of great entrepreneurship mindset. The corner shop operator and the grocer at the end of your street can be great entrepreneurs in their own ways and scales. It is about the mindset, the discipline, the resolve and on focus on what you do.

Last Word

Business Requirements

All through the book, I have tried to remind you that succeeding in business is about doing several things right, persistently, consistently and over an extended period. I have tried to bring out the issues that you need to think about and act on. Briefly, everything revolved around the following:

Intellectual capacity: In striving to create value, serve a customer group or groups and make money, you will need to constantly think through issues. You will need to come up with ideas and shape and refine them. You will need to come up with strategies and develop plans. You will need to be creative in raising cash as well as staying ahead of competition. These, you will find, are intellectually tasking activities.

Emotional intelligence: Understanding yourself as well as others, like your staff, customers, creditors, regulators, etc. is required for the success of your intelligent ideas. You will need to know how to manage yourself as well as your various relationships. Bottomline, you will need to be emotionally wise.

Bias for action: Business will throw up challenges and opportunities without regard to your personal conveniences. You must have the proclivity to seize opportunities and address challenges as they arise. None of the two factors mentioned above will help you succeed if you don't take actions as may be required.

In addition to the generalities above, as an entrepreneur you will also need to the following:

Continuous learning and self-development: An aspiring entrepreneur must be fast in developing, learning and adopting new concepts and good ideas. Frequently, you have to come up with your own new and novel ideas. Other times, you have to learn from others and adapt their ideas to your situation.

Reading books, travels, sharing ideas and experiences with other entrepreneurs, attending trade shows, fairs and events are all good ways of learning more and building on your knowledge and skills. If you are going into any new business, you have to learn pretty fast. If you are already in one, you have to keep learning, so as to keep ahead of your competition.

Take care of your relationships: Our relationships have a direct bearing on our wellbeing and true success. Whilst we are busy on legitimate business aspirations, we must remain alert and alive to our various relationships. At the end of everything, our material successes might not amount to much if we do not have healthy relationships and do not add positive value to the lives of others.

Take care of your health: Entrepreneurs exert themselves to the fullest mentally, physically and emotionally. The swings between different activities and emotions can be massive within short periods. These can all take a great toll on the health of the entrepreneur. Eating right, regular exercises, medical check-ups, etc. are all important if the entrepreneur is to be able to remain healthy and in a state to be able to continue to do the best they can.

Good luck!

Musbahu El Yakub

Index

About the Author

 Mr. El Yakub has worked at one of Nigeria's premier universities as a lecturer before going into banking where he rose to the level of a manager and head of branch. He also worked at one of the largest manufacturing corporations in Nigeria at senior executive levels.

Musbahu El Yakub holds a bachelor's and master's degrees in Nuclear Physics as well as a Master of Business Administration degree. He has attended several courses on credit management, corporate finance, corporate strategy, leadership, entrepreneurship, etc.

After his corporate career, Mr. El Yakub has been engaged as a serial entrepreneur, business and human capacity development consultant. He is passionate about entrepreneurship development in Nigeria and runs a blog, www.melyakub.com for Nigerian and African entrepreneurs as well as human capital development firm.

www.ingramcontent.com/pod-product-compliance
Lightning Source LLC
Chambersburg PA
CBHW071734150726

47998CB00005B/1634